LIBERATION
IN THE AMERICAS

Comparative Aspects of the Independence Movements
in Mexico and the United States

LIBERATION
IN THE AMERICAS

Comparative Aspects of the Independence Movements in Mexico and the United States

Edited by
Robert Detweiler and Ramón Ruiz

Border States Universities Consortium on Latin America
Occasional Publication Number Four

THE CAMPANILE PRESS
San Diego State University

Library of Congress Cataloging Data
Catalog Card no.: 77-83491
Detweiler, Robert and Ramon Ruiz, Eds.
Liberation in the Americas
San Diego, Calif.: Campanile Press, San Diego State University
p. x, 110
7708   770708

Hardback ISBN 0-916304-41-8
Paperback ISBN 0-916304-30-2

THE CAMPANILE PRESS
San Diego State University
San Diego, CA 92182

Foreword

THE CITY OF SAN DIEGO has a unique geographic position on the border with Mexico. As a result its people are constantly made aware of the city's heritage as an outpost of the Spanish Empire and as a gateway to the Mexican state of Baja California. Thus it was natural that when the city created a committee for its Bicentennial celebrations it was named the "Fronteras" committee. This spirit animated the meetings between the members of the departments of history at San Diego State University and the University of California, San Diego. During the initial meetings it was decided that the most appropriate way of celebrating the American independence movement was to view that experience in light of a similar experience in Mexico. This seemed doubly appropriate given the increasing contacts between the two sponsoring institutions and their sister institutions in northern Mexico. One manifestation of this relationship is the consortium of border universities that is sponsoring this volume.

The format chosen by the steering committee was a two-day conference with sessions on each campus featuring four invited historians. The committee was delighted to obtain the participation of four distinguished scholars. The first session was held at the University of California, San Diego with two featured speakers, Dr. Enrique Florescano and Dr. H. James Henderson. Enrique Florescano is the Assistant Director of the National Institute of Anthropology and History in Mexico City where he is also the head of the Department of Historical Investigations. He has edited various journals including the *Revista Historia Mexicana* and has also taught at the Colégio de México. Dr. Florescano is an economic historian who has written extensively on the agricultural history of New pain. This theme can be seen in such works as *Precios del Maíz y Crisis Agrícolas en México, 1709-1810* and *Estructuras y Problemas Agrícolas de México, 1520-1821*. Dr. H. James Henderson is a member of the department of history at Oklahoma State University. His work has concentrated on the origins of political parties during the struggle for independence and the years immediately following. This is best seen in his work *Political Parties in the Continentul Congress*. The second session of the symposium convened at San Diego State University. Leading off the session was Dr. Gary B. Nash of the University of California, Los Angeles. In his books *Quakers and Politics, Pennsylvania, 1681-1726* and *Red, White and Black*, and in many other works, Professor Nash has explored the process of social change and political interaction in the colonial and revolutionary periods. The final paper was delivered by Dr. Luis Villoro, a distinguished historian, philosopher, educator and political commentator. He has held a number of positions in the Universidad Nacional Autónoma de México and is currently Director of the Social Science and Humanities Division of the Universidad Autónoma Metropolitana. Besides his many works on philosophy, Dr. Villoro has explored the ideological background to the Mexican independence movement in his *El Proceso Ideológico de la Revolución de Independencia*.

"Liberation in the Americas: Comparative Independence Movements in Mexico and the United States" could not have succeeded without assistance from many sources. Chancellor William B. McElroy of UCSD and Vice-President Trevor Colbourn of SDSU provided the financing. Dr. Colbourn has written extensively on the American Revolution and was an active participant in the meetings. Dr. Ramón Eduardo Ruiz and Dr. Douglas Strong, chairmen respectively of the history departments at UCSD and SDSU, hosted the sessions. Others such as Robert Detweiler, Earl Pomeroy, Paul Vanderwood, Michael Monteón, and Alejandra Patterson helped make the conference a success.

Robert C. Ritchie

CONTENTS

Introduction

Robert Detweiler
and
Ramón Ruiz

WITH THE EXCEPTION of Canada and the new Caribbean nations, the republics of the Western Hemisphere won their independence with armed struggles against the mother country. The Thirteen Colonies, maturing offspring of England, led the way; New Spain, eventually the Republic of Mexico and one of the leading viceroyalites of the Iberian empire, followed less than half a century later. Between 1783, when the Peace of Paris granted English Americans their freedom, and 1821, when Mexico broke with Spain, most of the former Spanish colonies embarked on political paths of their own. Common principles and aspirations united the nascent republics. Yet, in diverse ways, a huge chasm set aside the heritage of the new Spanish American republics from their neighbor to the north, the fledgling United States. Separated by a historical past often at odds with the English experience, the offspring of Spain faced a future markedly different. Still, as scholars acknowledge, the European rulers who molded the colonial framework of the young republics had shared a continent and similar values for centuries.

Given the paradox of comparable historical roots which ultimately produced divergent results in the New World, scholars ask if the Americas enjoy a common history. The debate has held sway for over a generation, inspired in part by the seminal work of Herbert E. Bolton. In his famous address before the American Historical Association in 1932, Bolton had urged historians to bridge national boundaries and view the Western Hemisphere as an entity. Particularly during the colonial period, he maintained, the common features of the various New World societies transcended the cultural differences of the European powers they represented. The Spanish, Portuguese, French, English, and Dutch each built similar colonial systems and imposed roughly the same mercantilistic restraints. Each had to contend with native American populations. Each introduced slavery in its provinces. Each transferred neo-feudal institutions that gradually adjusted to conditions in the New World.

However, most scholars today are skeptical of Bolton's thesis. True, European nations responded to similar imperial opportunities in the New World and generally dealt with the same challenges, but it is dangerous to overemphasize the common heritage of the Americas. Most agree that the search for a common history is less rewarding than a comparative approach that recognizes at the outset diversities as well as the similarities among New World communities. Such an hypothesis offers a framework for greater understanding, and it is from this perspective that the colonial liberation movements that led to the establishment of the United States in 1776 and of Mexico in 1821 should be studied.

Obviously, Mexican and North American independence share much in common. In both instances, New World colonists struck for control over their own destinies after generations of imperial rule. Both movements were fertilized by similar forces at work in the second half of the eighteenth century. Both were built on or were rationalized by ideas of the Enlightenment. Both were successful. The similarities are there, but so too are striking contrasts.

The contrasts are, in large part, a reflection of the respective colonial societies that spawned the independence movements. The Spaniards who conquered the lands of the Aztecs and the English who slowly settled the north Atlantic seaboard came from societies engulfed by two distinct processes of change. Differences in time of settlement magnified these differences between Spain and England. The Spanish-American colonies were launched in the early sixteenth century and reflected the medieval character of their mother country. But a full century intervened before the English began to carve out a New World empire, a century that witnessed a major transformation of English society. Further, the English underwent a religious transformation and broke with the Roman Catholic hierarchy. They launched the beginnings of a modern capitalistic economy and developed the classic bourgeois values of thrift and industry. They began to transform their traditional monarchy and to develop a parliamentary system.

It is not merely a matter of comparing two traditions when analyzing New Spain and the Thirteen Colonies, but of contrasting a traditional culture with one in the state of flux. From the start, the English experience in the New World differed sharply from that of the Spaniards. Whereas Spain acted swiftly and boldly to carve out a huge New World domain, the English moved slowly and indecisively. Spain's conquistadores led a rapid campaign of exploration and conquest of the vast new lands and native peoples. By the time the English had established their first feeble settlement at Jamestown in 1607, some fifty years after their first landings, Spain's empire already extended nearly 8,000 miles from California to the Straits of Magellan. Indeed, Spain held dominion over the largest empire the Western world had known since the fall of Rome. By almost any measure the vast Spanish empire dwarfed the English imperial efforts.

Almost from the start, America yielded tremendous wealth to the Spaniards, while the English tasted none of these fabulous riches. Indeed, for the first half century or more, the English colonial investors realized few if any profits from their American enterprises. Also, unlike Spain, England's government maintained a low profile in imperial affairs, refusing to give substantial support to colony builders. True, the English monarchs granted charters to groups or individuals willing to risk their personal fortunes in colonization efforts, but they accepted none of the burden of financing colonies and left most of the responsibility for government to the entrepreneurs of settlement and the colonists themselves. The Spanish government, on the other hand, helped finance and attempted to rigidly control its colonies from the outset.

Both the Spaniards and the English found native Americans in their New World lands. But there were significant differences between the Indians in the two areas and equally significant responses in the ways the two European groups dealt with them. The Spanish conquerors encountered the Aztecs and Incas who lived in great numbers in highly sophisticated societies characterized by advanced economies and complex religious, political, and cultural institutions. The Spaniards attempted to Hispanicize these natives and to incorporate them into their colonial society. But the British met relatively small populations of Indians who lived in comparatively primitive cultures. Neither the British government nor the settlers attempted to absorb these natives into their social fabric. Conquest for the English meant the devastation of Indian communities and pushing surviving natives westward, seemingly the easiest solution. Spain Christianized the natives and gave them a place in Spanish American society, albeit often a place at the bottom of the totem pole. The Spaniards, in short, managed to order their society in such a way as to make the Indians a part of it, while the English felt compelled to repopulate their New World territories with Europeans and African slaves.

There were other distinctions. The English made no attempt to control the migration of Europeans to their colonies as did Spain. Aside from African slaves, who were brought in to supply labor, only Spaniards were allowed in the Spanish colonies as their government tightly regulated the emigration of Spaniards as well. Spain attempted to send over noblemen, clergymen, tradesmen, and farmers in numbers roughly equivalent to their proportion of the population at home. The English, on the other hand, encouraged the trade in Africans and the great migration of non-English Europeans, especially during the eighteenth century. Indeed, in the period 1700 to 1776 non-English emigrants outnumbered colonists from the British Isles by a wide margin. Some 50,000 Germans entered the colony of Pennsylvania alone between 1727 and 1740. By the time of the War for Independence, sizeable populations of Dutch, Germans, Swedes, French, Welsh, Scots, Swiss, Scotch-Irish, Jews and other non-English Europeans dotted Anglo America from Maine to Georgia. Unlike Spanish America, the North American colonies sheltered a mixture of nationalities to be found in no other place in the world.

A wide range of Protestant sects made their home in the English colonies. Dissenting Protestants saw Anglo America as a refuge where they could worship unmolested. By 1776 the British colonies were replete with Presbyterians, Congregationalists, Moravians, Baptists, Quakers, Anglicans and, on occasion, even Catholics and Jews. No single church could claim more than 17 percent of the total population. In New Spain, by contrast, the Catholic Church was totally dominant. Spanish law expressly barred dissenters and heretics of all kinds from emigrating to America and, in time,

Spanish America became a stronghold of Catholic orthodoxy nearly equal to Spain itself.

One important contrast between the colonial societies was in social structure. Spanish America presented an infinite variety of colors, classes and castes, a structure rigidly stratified and immobile with a tiny, but all-powerful, elite, in the majority white, at the top. In sharp contrast, English colonial society was comparatively classless, mobile and, with the exception of the slaves, overwhelmingly white. Europeans in the English colonies had a unique opportunity to achieve higher status. The relative ease of acquiring land and the economic, social, and political status that went with it tended to make Anglo America a mobile community. Aside from the black slaves, about one person in five by 1776, most North Americans were caught up in a social system distinguished by its flexibility. There were opportunities for lowly servants to ascend the social ladder; an ambitious worker could learn a skill, enter a trade, buy land, or set up shop for himself. Few well-to-do came to the English colonies. Mostly the ambitious poor or lower middle-classes ventured across the Atlantic with the hope of getting a plot of private land. From one-half to two-thirds of those who came to the English colonies were bond servants who labored for a number of years before achieving freedom. Farmers, tenants, and farm laborers, attracted by the promise of cheap or free land, soon formed a largely middle-class society. There was no hereditary nobility, although a new native "aristocracy" or highly influential upper class of great planters and successful merchants eventually commanded the social structure. But this upper element was generally open to any who had the success and property to qualify. Compared to the rigid stratification of Europe or Spanish America, the colonial English enjoyed a more open society.

Only a limited degree of private enterprise existed in New Spain, no more than in the Old World. In the English colonies, however, there was no fixed pattern into which business had to fit, no powerful interests to which it was required to adjust. There was no powerful monarchy, no universal church, no landed aristocracy, no army, no guilds, and few legal restraints on free enterprise. Spain, conversely, attempted to manipulate the economic life of its colonies. Almost from the beginning, the land fell into the hands of landlords, which meant that the masses had little opportunity for upward mobility.

The widespread distribution of private land among white men in the English colonies encouraged a political structure and tradition that contrasted with that in the Spanish New World. In time men with property—freeholders—came to dominate local government in the counties and towns of Anglo America and they alone voted for representatives to what were eventually to be the most powerful centers of provincial administration, the assemblies.

From the outset, the charters of the trading companies, which founded the original colonies, provided for an organization that was basically self-directing. The stockholders were authorized to meet and to elect officers and enact the rules and regulations of the company. As early as 1619, the English colonists began consciously to model their rules and procedures of government after those of the House of Commons. In a brief span, the idea of a representative legislature became an integral part of the government of each of the colonies. These colonial legislatures gained increasing power over the governors and other officers of the British home government. The key to the growing independence of the colonial assemblies was their control over finances. Only the elected representatives of the colonists could tax, which meant that the assemblies were able to use the power of the purse to seize substantial political power. They determined the salaries of officials, appointed judges and local administrative officers, regulated

Indian affairs, controlled military affairs, supervised the churches, and taxed the citizens.

The British home government was generally tolerant concerning the growing power of the colonial assemblies. The complex of imperial agencies and officials was little more than a thin overlay imposed on the semi-independent provincial governments. For example, the British home government reserved the right to disallow colonial laws, but in practice it rarely exercised this power. Of the 8,500 laws submitted for approval to the Privy Council in London, only 470 or about 5.5 percent were disallowed and often the bureaucracy of review was so slow that the laws had already served their purpose in America before they were ever considered in England.

The Anglo-American assemblies had usurped virtually all the important powers of government by the mid-eighteenth century. They were controlled by rising provincial elites placed in power by the votes of the freeholders or large middle-class of white men with property. The numbers of voters was exceptionally high. Because land was easy to acquire and ownership of a few acres qualified a white man to vote, the North American colonists had a higher proportion of their population qualified to vote than any contemporary society in the world. The advances toward self-government were not necessarily planned or even consciously undertaken. There was no master plan to grasp the power of the empire. But the unplanned effect of more than a century of quiet political struggle between the assemblies and the forces of royal government was virtual political autonomy for the colonials and their firm belief in the right to govern themselves. On the eve of the War for Independence, English Americans were exercising self-government and were fully prepared for self-determination once the power of the mother country disappeared. The struggle for English Americans was less a war to achieve self-rule than one to preserve the political autonomy they had long since practiced.

Conditions of local government in Spanish America stood in sharp contrast. Despite the vastness of their empire, the Spaniards displayed remarkable skill in administering it as a coherent, well-organized unit. Their elaborate imperial bureaucracy was based on a hierarchical structure where ultimate authority rested with the monarch of Castile, a patriarchal figure whose control of the provinces was viewed as an extension of his personal dynastic power. The highest regulatory agency for the colonies in Spain, the Council of the Indies, ruled in the king's name. It exercised jurisdiction over all matters in America, both secular and religious, issuing all laws and decrees and appointing all officials who executed these regulations.

To administer the almost limitless expanse of the Spanish empire, the Council of the Indies created huge viceroyalties. The viceroy of New Spain, whose jurisdiction was first established in 1535 and included the entire area of Spanish America north of Panama, was delegated great powers. The viceroyalty was, in turn, divided into four audiencias, giant administrative subdivisions that were further divided in a series of complex administrative units down to the *cabildo,* the lowest unit of civil government for urban areas. The audiencias or the viceroy appointed each officer in these various subdivisions, subject to the approval of the Council of the Indies in Spain. The hierarchy was quite precise, a coherent state system whose ultimate authority flowed from the monarchs in the mother country. To assure its control, the Crown overlaid imperial hierarchy with investigating and superintending agencies which scrutinized American governmental affairs.

The Spanish royal government managed to control its sprawling empire for three hundred years with a precision that was never approached in the Anglo-American colonies. The power of the Spanish monarchs penetrated deep into the daily lives of their subjects. There were imperfections in this model of hierarchical authority, of course, especially in remote reaches of the empire where local authorities frequently managed to ignore the directives of their superiors. But resistance to unpopular policies or offensive officials usually took the form of evasion or passive refusal to comply rather than open, organized opposition to the state. Yet, paradoxically, with the decline in vigor of the mother country, Spanish Americans, like their English neighbors to the north, had managed to win a measure of freedom from intervention by royal officials by 1810.

Still, the Spanish Americans never mounted a sustained, coherent effort to build independent governments during their long colonial tutelage. They articulated no concrete body of ideas to justify opposition to the crown, and no leaders appeared to challenge the authority of the royal structure until late. When the Spanish empire began to collapse, no corps of native politicians able to design and manage stable self-governments had appeared on the scene. English Americans, by contrast, had never been subject to an effective imperial government and were able to mount opposition to the state and to organize local self-rule. The authority of the English monarchs and the Parliament was scattered over a half dozen uncoordinated governmental agencies whose function was frequently superficial. Controls over trade and customs were relatively effective, but there was little royal control over the growing independent American political system. By the mid-seventeenth century there was organized resistance to the agents of royal authority and by the mid-eighteenth century English Americans had developed their own corps of political leaders and semi-independent local governments. The colonial assemblies were the most important instruments for executing policy at the provincial level, but the degree of self-rule ran much deeper. Equally important were the governments of the towns and counties, which were quite independent of central control and handled local taxation, justice, land titles, licensing of businesses, planning of roads, poor relief, elementary education, and virtually all other matters. By 1776 resistance to royal government was quite sophisticated and the tradition of local self-rule nearly complete. There was leadership and a foundation for self-government that made the transition to independence comparatively smooth.

Spanish Americans, too, had opportunities to develop bases for independent political institutions. But the institutions that might have matured into local centers of competition with the central state never flourished. In the earliest years of the Spanish empire, for example, the crown granted extraordinary powers to the *adelantados*, feudal lords with unconfined authority to bring the frontier under control. But the adelantados withered after the second generation. Similarly, the *encomenderos*, who received grants of Indians to till their lands, were a potential power base. But by the early seventeenth century they were no longer a possible source of political opposition. There was also the possibility that the Spanish provincial assemblies, periodic meetings of municipal leaders to raise funds or introduce new policies, might have evolved into popular legislatures. These provincial assemblies had the potential to grow into parliamentary bodies in the tradition of the Spanish Cortes much as the British colonial assemblies replicated the House of Commons. But this never occurred in the Spanish communities. A similar fate befell the cabildos or town councils.

The reasons are not entirely clear why these semi-independent agencies in Spanish America failed to mature when similar ones in British America grew rapidly into a condition of provincial political self-direction. Part of the explanation must lie in the fact that the Spanish monarchy took a much more active role in colonial affairs than the British monarchy. The British crown did little more than encourage private colonizers to settle North America, while the Spaniards asserted absolute royal authority in America. The Catholic Church fully supported the assertion of royal authority, and there was no competing body of ideas. The entire political culture of Spain and of Spanish America upheld the doctrine of royal supremacy.

Another important part of the explanation seems to relate to the significant differences in class structure and population characteristics between Spanish and English America. Whereas North American society was dominated by a large middle-class of white landholders who had won the right to political participation, in Spanish America a small elite of Europeans and upper-class mestizos controlled the lives of the countless poor, usually of Indian descent and always landless peasants or subsistence farmers.

At the pinnacle of Spanish-American society stood a small group of imperial officers, including the viceroys, audiencia judges, provincial governors, numerous officials of the Church, and a host of lesser imperial appointees. These men, the most powerful in the social order, might have gradually developed a tradition of local independent government had they not been so closely attached to Spain and controlled by the royal system. But unlike the British provinces, where American-born colonists held nearly all the positions of local political leadership, almost all high officers of state and the Church in the Spanish colonies were peninsular Spaniards, men born and reared in Spain who did not identify with colonial interests and who planned to return to Spain after completing their assignments in America. In the entire 300 years of Spanish colonial government only four viceroys, and fourteen of the 602 other high civil officers whose careers have been traced were born in America. Similarly, the leaders of the Church were also primarily from peninsular Spain. Of 706 bishops and archbishops who served in the Spanish-American colonies, 601 were born in Spain.

Meanwhile, the Council of the Indies instituted various controls to ensure that crown officials would not use their positions to develop independent authority. Their tenure in office was strictly limited; they were regularly transferred from one post to another within the empire to prevent too strong an identification with any particular local area; they were kept dependent on the royal treasury for their salaries; and various boards and agencies were maintained to review and scrutinize their conduct in office. For the most part, the powerful class of imperial leaders at the top of Spanish-American society never developed the desire or the wherewithal to oppose vigorously royal authority.

The segment of the Spanish-American society that conceivably could have initiated a vigorous challenge to royal supremacy was the Creoles, men of Spanish descent born in America. But the Creoles were never more than a thin veneer of the population of Spanish America, unlike the situation in the British colonies where Americans of European descent made up more than 80 percent of the total population. While the British encouraged emigration to Anglo America, the Spaniards restricted emigration to their provinces. In the entire 300 years of colonial rule, only about 300,000 Spaniards emigrated to New Spain. By contrast, some 200,000 settlers left the British Isles for North America in the first 50 years of settlement alone, and in the eighteenth century thousands flocked there from various parts of Europe. Because the Creoles constituted only a tiny fraction of the total population, they were closely tied to Spain; they identified with the mother country as the source of their status and political power. The fact that they were of European descent and distinguished racially from the mass of Spanish Americans also determined their social status and identification as part of the ruling class. Consequently their basic interests were generally with Spain and they chose not to engage in vigorous opposition to royal authority. A minority of influential mestizos took its cue from the Creoles and Spaniards.

The rest of Spanish-American society, the bulk of the population not of pure European blood, was never in a position to challenge the power of the central state system. The largest segment of the population, the peasants of Indian descent, were rapidly reduced to a mass incapable of organizing its own political institutions. Similarly, blacks and the bulk of the mestizos were socially inferior to the dominant Spanish elements, and social pressures prevented them from asserting themselves effectively in politics. For the most part, the mass of Indians, blacks, mulattos and mestizos lacked the freedom, self-esteem, and experience to devise effective political weapons against the overwhelming Spanish establishment. The peninsular Spaniards were tied to royal supremacy, and the Creoles, surrounded by Indians, blacks, and the racially mixed, depended on a continuing identification with Spain as the source of their status. Thus none of the major segments of Spanish-American society was prepared to develop vigorous independent political institutions. As a consequence, when the people of the Spanish colonies created independent nations in the nineteenth century, they had not yet acquired the institutions or the experience of self-rule to move smoothly into nationhood. This is perhaps the most important point of contrast respecting the independence movements in Spanish and English America.

Both movements for independence, nonetheless, were largely an effort to protect gains won earlier. For rebellious English Americans it was an attempt to maintain the relatively independent status and condition of local self-rule that upper and middle-class Americans of European descent enjoyed under imperial rule. In the period after 1763, when the British home government moved to limit provincial autonomy, the dissident colonists chose to resist. Ultimately, they resorted to rebellion to preserve what they had gained during a century and a half of colonial life. By the same token, the minority of rebellious Creoles who challenged Spanish authority, did so to keep their hard-won privileges. This was particularly so of the higher clergy and the officer elite in the colonial militias; both groups looked with jaundiced eye upon the crown's attempt in 1820 to revamp the colonial structure.

Despite the crown's attempts to keep for itself both political and economic power, local elites in Spanish America had staked out areas of influence and wealth. The Creoles appear to have held extensive local power particularly in the cabildos; the attempt of the Spanish government to curtail it in the late colonial period encouraged the Creole elite to fight for independence. Like the elites in English colonies, the Creoles sought to preserve their economic and political status by rebelling against the mother country. In the first essay in this volume, Luis Villoro notes that in the latter half of the eighteenth century the home governments of both the English and Spanish Americans attempted to increase political dependency and to strengthen economic controls. In both the British colonies and New Spain, the provincial elites led and supported the independence movements.

Villoro, however, is quick to point out important distinctions between the elites in the two movements. He suggests that in the Thirteen Colonies they were attempting to maintain a popular power already in existence while in Mexico they were trying to sustain a state of social privilege for themselves and to deny power to the common people. A fundamental difference between the two independence movements, according to Villoro, lies in the fact that North American society was relatively free from poverty and had fewer class distinctions than any other society. But in New Spain the elite, which favored independence, had to confront a miserable underclass dispossessed of almost all rights. From this basic difference, he maintains, the United States was born without the tradition of social revolution that has characterized Mexico from the beginning.

Although compared to New Spain the Anglo-Americans were relatively free of class distinctions, this is not to suggest that their society was without its underclass. As Gary B. Nash points out in the second essay, the part played by this underclass, especially the blacks and Indians, is overlooked. He believes that the American Revolution was more than a struggle by principled colonists to protect their political authority against a tyrannical mother country. It was, for many blacks and Indians, a struggle for liberty and genuine revolutionary change. It was frequently a struggle fought on the side of the British *against* the revolutionists. Not all of the common people of North America supported independence nor were they all satisfied with the character of the social order.

In the third essay, Enrique Florescano concentrates on the social inequities in New Spain at the time of independence. He contends that the period of rapid economic growth in New Spain in the late eighteenth and early nineteenth centuries, accompanied by the Bourbon reforms, accelerated social disequilibrium. There was a widespread economic boom but the distribution of benefits was quite unequal, which exacerbated old inequities. The imperial structure lacked the channels of social mobility and the political flexibility that might have absorbed the tensions that resulted. This condition, coupled with the dissemination of fresh ideas, not only encouraged alienated groups to move for independence from Spain but implanted a tradition of social revolution for Mexico.

The final essay by H. James Henderson illustrates that the British Americans shared with Mexico and other nations emerging from successful independence movements the problem of reconciling local and sectional differences into a manageable political system. His study of the Continental Congress traces the efforts to nationalize

American politics and stresses the regional strains that accompanied the independence movement as its leaders struggled to weld together a nation of disparate parts. His regional comparison coincides with Villoro's and Florescano's studies of Mexico in that it suggests that broad generalizations about colonial societies in the act of achieving independence can be misleading, since within each colonial society there are many different types of settlements which, in themselves, present strong contrasts.

These studies confirm that under close scrutiny we can trace both similarities and striking disparities between the colonial liberation movements of the Americas. These parallels and divergencies reflect, in large part, the cultural differences of the respective European imperial nations and the conditions of the colonial societies they built in the Western Hemisphere. Such comparisons provide insight not only into the degree to which the Americas have a common history, but also increase our understanding of the history of both the United States and Mexico by widening our perspective and suggesting new areas for analysis.

1

Mexican and North American Independence: Parallels and Divergences

Luis Villoro

To COMPARE TWO HISTORICAL MOVEMENTS as diverse as the independence movements of Mexico and North America would appear at the outset a task condemned to generalities, and ultimately of scant value. Yet, a comparison could prove worthwhile if its goal is not to become bogged down in common realities, but to take off from there and point out the fundamental differences. The distinctiveness of each process is better understood by comparing it against common characteristics shared with other similar processes. After all, is it not the task of history to gain knowledge of the specific through the general?°

In the second half of the eighteenth century, in the colonies of North America as well as in New Spain, the features of dependency and exploitation in the policies of both metropolitan governments worsened. Mercantilist ideas, which advocated greater intervention of the State in economic matters, gained ground in England and Spain. Both countries moved toward a greater administrative centralization and developed a more conscious policy of control of colonial production and tried to increase the economic benefits derived from America.

In the thirteen colonies of North America, this turn in English policy was evidenced in a dramatic event; Parliament approved the Stamp Act, which imposed unaccustomed tax measures on the colonies. Until then England had maintained a somewhat liberal and permissive economic policy in her colonies. Without doubt, there existed statutes which restricted the local production of manufactured articles which England exported. These affected, for example, woolen cloth, hats, and iron goods. However, there was freedom of production and commerce in the majority of areas. Foreign commerce was regulated by the Navigation Acts, but these were not strongly enforced, and in practice allowed widespread contraband, and even favored the maritime commercial participation of northern colonial enterprises. Because of this, they never engendered open rebellion on the part of the colonists. Only the promulgation of taxes on sugar, in 1733, the so-called Molasses Act, provoked strong discontent, but this decree was never applied effectively.

° A slightly different version of this essay previously appeared in Spanish in the Mexican periodical, *Plural*. The translation is by Rosalie Schwartz.

This liberal Crown policy appeared destined for the scrap heap in 1763. The Stamp Act, the most obvious measure, seemed to English Americans an alarming first step. Tied to the Stamp Act were other similar measures. The metropolis tried to reinvigorate the Molasses Act, reinforce control over foreign navigation and utilize a royal fleet to end contraband. Other measures were interpreted easily as attempts to reinforce central power. England decided to maintain an expanded military in the colonies and proposed to establish an American episcopate. Finally, the Townsend Acts, by establishing new taxes on imports and trade, made the new interventionist policy obvious.

This policy affected principally the interests of the colonial elite, merchants, and property owners. The first feared new regulations on commerce, including the intervention of Parliament in the promotion of monopolies. The landowners, already burdened by large debts, were not disposed to bear additional exactions. But if the reaction in the colonies was violent, it was because these measures were interpreted as a substitution by the metropolis of its previous permissive attitude with one of imposition and regulation of production and commerce.

Similarly, in the same decade, Spain carried out a notable change in policy towards its colonies. In 1765, two years after the approval of the Stamp Act, José de Gálvez was named *Visitador de Indias* (Inspector), charged with implementing a new policy of tax control. The composition of the society of New Spain was quite different from that of the thirteen colonies, however, and therefore the repercussions of this policy were quite distinct.

The economy of New Spain was not based on individual proprietors who produced freely for internal consumption, but on the exploitation of mining and on a commercial sector geared to financing the production of precious metals and their subsequent export to the metropolis. One of the aims of the new policy was to protect and reinforce this sector. In the second half of the eighteenth century, particularly after 1770, mining experienced a tremendous boom. Between 1740 and 1803 the quantity of gold and silver extracted from the mines of New Spain tripled. This enormous growth in mining was accompanied by a correspondent bonanza for the commercial houses which managed foreign trade. The greatest fortunes in the colony were found in one or the other of these two groups. Foreign commerce was controlled by a few firms, situated primarily in Mexico City or Veracruz, which maintained tight relations with concerns in Cádiz, Spain. The decree of *comercio libre*, or free trade, of 1778, which lifted prohibitions so that New Spain might trade with other American countries, encouraged, in the long run, the establishment of new commercial firms and benefitted the richest wholesalers. In the first decade of the nineteenth century, the Veracruz trade almost doubled in relation to 1778. In those years the export sector had managed to consolidate itself at the top of the economic ladder. Many of their fortunes were intimately connected to those of the mine owners. The export merchants constituted the best source of mining credit. The so-called *aviadores* (middlemen), who purchased the metal from the miners in order to export it and often extended the credit which the miners needed, had their accounts in the great commercial houses of Mexico City. Other commercial houses served as bankers directly to the mines and thus controlled a good part of the extractive industry. Miners and exporters formed the economically dominant group in the last era of the colony. This group's hegemony was tied to the maintenance of an "enclave" economy, as its greatest profit derived from exports to the metropolis. Its privileged position was inseparable from a condition of dependence.

However, this bolstering of the export sector in the second half of the eighteenth century also encouraged a slow increase in the productive sector tied to the internal market, which was not favored by royal policy. Indeed, the colonial elite contained other groups which viewed the economic policy of the metropolis with distrust. First, there were the great rural landowners. A great deal of the land was distributed in smaller holdings and Indian communities with low productivity, reduced almost to subsistence. There existed, however, some 5,000 large estates that produced for a national—or at least, regional—market. The process of concentration in the hands of a few creole estate owners was growing. Between the years 1779 and 1810, the *hacendados* had gained increasing profits, thanks to the continuous rise in the price of corn. However, the conditions for the accumulation of capital in the agrarian sector were elusive. Not only were the profits obtained relative to invested capital quite inferior to those in mining, they were subject to the cyclical fluctuations of agricultural prices, an ill from which the economy of the Viceroyalty could never free itself. The majority lived perpetually in debt, properties encumbered as collateral for long-term credit. The finance capital on which it depended was in the hands of an institution which, in addition to controlling great rural properties, acted as agrarian banker—the Church.

The Church held many properties, in the countryside as well as in the city. But its principal economic base consisted of capital in private properties. The Church administered close to 45 million pesos through its chaplaincies and pious funds. Each chaplaincy court, each religious brotherhood, was a type of bank. They loaned to the hacendados, to the industrialists, and to the small merchants extensive capital at moderate interest and on long terms. A strong economic interdependence existed between Church and hacendados. The Church extended vital credit to the landowners, above all in years of crisis. Through mortgages the Church controlled a great number of rural properties. The clergy thus constituted a social group whose economic interests were directed to the internal market of the colony. In this sense, they were bound together with the agricultural and industrial proprietors, and the small merchants.

The general economic boom which derived from the growth in mineral production, the relative liberation of internal trade fostered by the Bourbons and, above all from the closing of the market to the products coming from Spain due to the continual wars in which the metropolis was involved, had encouraged an incipient production of consumer goods destined for the internal market. The textile industry, which produced coarse cotton cloth, developed considerably in Tlaxcala and Puebla, as did the production of woolen blankets in Querétaro, Celaya, San Miguel, and Saltillo. Various other industries also developed: leather, furniture, soap, hats, pottery, and shoes. In spite of prohibitions and monopolies, the wine and tobacco industries thrived. In some regions light industry began to have a considerable importance and to replace imports.

These sectors, then, were the ones affected by the growing interventionism of the metropolis in the colonial economy. If in North America the legal restraints against local production were strongly resented only after 1763, in New Spain the offenses were much older. Indeed, the Crown had established thousands of legal measures which impeded the consolidation and expansion of the internal productive sector. To avoid competition with the Spaniards, they expressly prohibited many industries. They ordered destroyed textile factories which produced articles competing with those from Spain; in particular, they closed down the silk industry. The factories which survived were burdened with stringent laws. In addition, the numerous state monopolies, which extended to such diverse materials as tobacco, salt, and playing cards, hindered the free investment of capital in many lines. The expansion of the market found itself obstructed by a complex system of customs, tariffs and sales taxes which retarded trade and increased the cost of products considerably.

If all of these measures had been followed to the letter, nascent industry would have been stifled. However, the dispositions were not always respected. The restraints were often more formal than real. The legislative theory was not applicable against the force with which the economy of New Spain began to develop, in spite of the law. In short, in New Spain as in North America, the economic reality is found to be, in fact, far ahead of what was foreseen by the legislation, which never successfully impeded material progress. There existed a disjunction between the legislative and administrative spheres, resulting from the situation of dependence and the economic base. Because it did not parallel the advance of production, the legislation became a useless hindrance.

A dramatic expression of this dislocation was the stringent tax policy established by the Crown precisely when the growth of production for an internal market demanded the abolition of restraints. In the Thirteen Colonies, the rebellion justifiably came to rest under the banner "no taxation without representation," which symbolized the rejection of the tax policy. Without achieving the same political force, a similar reaction was provoked in New Spain. After 1786, a new administrative apparatus, controlled directly by the metropolis, was established: the so-called system of *intendencias* or administrative areas, designed to maintain strict control over the collection of taxes. The increase in taxes affected chiefly the sector with diminished capacity for accumulation of capital: hacendados, clergy, and incipient industrial manufacturers. The tax reform paid enormous dividends to the Crown. Nearly ten million pesos began to flow annually to Spain through imposition of taxes. At the beginning the the nineteenth century, New Spain was supplying the metropolis with three-fourths of all its revenues from the colonies.

One of the groups which suffered most from this drain was the Church, and with it the hacendados and industrialists who depended upon it for credit. The men of property in New Spain never stopped protesting this policy of exploitation and continual taxation. The city council of Mexico City, beginning with its *Representación* of 1771, as well as the representatives of the high clergy, repeatedly solicited the reduction of taxes, the supression of the laws against production, and the abolition of restraints which blocked the expansion of the market. All was in vain. Not only were they not heeded, but the response dealt a blow against the economy of New Spain: on December 26, 1804, a royal decree ordered the nationalization of all the capital of the chaplaincies and pious funds and demanded that mortgages be called up, and the estates sold where credit was forfeited. The money obtained was to be sent to the metropolis. The measure had already been applied in Spain, with advantageous results for the Crown, but in the colony the situation was different. Half of the agriculture was in the hands of hacendados who had for the most part mortgaged their properties. The application of the decree would put them on the edge of ruin. Protest groups came into existence in all areas of the country, asking for the revocation of the decree. The landowners of México, Pátzcuaro, Tehuacán, Valladolid, the councils of the cities of México, Valladolid, and Puebla, even the Mining Court, which had not been directly affected, sent dramatic *representaciones* to the Crown. Only the merchant's guild of the city of México, which represented the great export merchants, and some European bishops, supported the Viceroy in defense of the decree.

Despite all the protests, the royal decree was enforced, with disastrous effects. Through application of the law, New Spain turned over to the Royal Treasury some ten to twelve million pesos. The internal economy of the colony suffered terribly from the plunder. The Church and the rural property owners, particularly the middle and small owners, were naturally the most greatly affected. Many estates were sold for a pittance and innumerable small holders were bankrupted. Investments were withdrawn in all economic sectors which did not depend on exports.

At the end of the eighteenth century and the beginning of the nineteenth, New Spain suffered markedly from the structure of dependence. Within the elite the interests of two distinct sectors tended increasingly to diverge. On one side were the groups which had consolidated power and were closely bound to the system of dependency: miners, exporters, bureaucrats; on the other the sectors interested in promoting an internal market: the Church, the great landowners, provincial merchants, and nascent industrialists. If indeed these groups benefitted also from the general prosperity, they suffered more than any other the restraints and exactions imposed by the system. It is not odd that they began to consider themselves the victims of exploitation. Not surprisingly, their attitudes tended to be antagonistic toward the export sector. Their privileged position impelled them to maintain the social order and to safeguard it from any hint of instability. However, they became increasingly more aware of the political and legal obstacles blocking their progress. The annoyances which the legal restraints caused them, and the lack of understanding which the Crown demonstrated, pushed them toward reformist attitudes, guided by a central goal: a political and legislative structure in accord with the economic situation of the colony.

This divergence of interests between the sectors which made up the economic oligarchy of the colonies explains the divergent attitudes in the independence movement. In the English colonies the royalists did not coincide with a sector clearly defined by specific economic interests, and the majority of the elite ultimately accepted an attitude favorable to independence. In New Spain the oligarchy found itself divided. The dominant group, dependent upon the export sector, became the bitter defender of the condition of dependency; the other privileged sectors, on the other hand, supported changing positions which parallel those of the North American elite. In 1808, they advocated a process of political reform which might have led to independence, without changing the social order of the colony. Later, after a violent popular rebellion broke out in 1810, they opposed the movement for fear of the lower classes, even though they maintained their reformist ideas. With the popular rebellion put down, they encouraged an independence on their own terms in 1821.

II

It might be thought-provoking, therefore, to establish some parallels between the attitude and political mentality of that sector of New Spain and those which prevailed in the North American elite, but not in concrete political doctrines or in philosophical influences. These are, as a matter of fact, quite different. In the North American colonies, the enlightened, democratic lines of thought, which found their sources in Locke and Montesquieu, prevailed. In New Spain the doctrines were others: Suárez and the political thought of the Jesuits, rational natural law (Puffendorf, Heinecio), and the liberal Spanish tradition. Only after the outbreak of the popular rebellion, upon the radicalization of the movement, did the thought of the Enlightenment and the influence of the French Revolution become dominant, but even then this current was not able to win over all members of the elite.

The parallel is more formal. It refers to common historical attitudes, to a general mentality which can be expressed in distinct political doctrines. This is not surprising, since both groups were located in similar social situations within their respective countries and responded to similar challenges.

In the English colonies, the central ideas of independence thought could be summarized in a few brief propositions:

(1) The equality of the colonies with England was based on the existing juridical order, which conceded to the Americans the same rights as English citizens. Since the so-called "Glorious Revolution" of 1688, in the opinion of many Americans an established constitutional principle had united the advantages of monarchy, aristocracy, and democracy, and

affirmed definitively the liberties and rights of all the English. The pretensions of the Americans rested on the same constitution. They did not subvert the legal order, but on the contrary, appealed to the tradition from which sprang the liberties of Britain itself. Moreover, they could be extended back to their origins in the Middle Ages. Thus, John Adams could cite the Magna Carta to support them.

(2) From this juridical tradition sprang the thesis that the colonies were nations with the same autonomy and privileges as England. It was a matter of a confederation of independent states united under one head. They owed allegiance, therefore, only to the King, but not to the British Parliament; as the colonies were not dependencies of the people of England, neither were the latter dependencies of the American people. In this sense, the Thirteen Colonies defended a *status* of liberty which already existed and did not claim to gain a new one.

(3) This liberty, this equality with the people of England, was expressed in an existing popular power: the representative assemblies of the states. The Lower Houses were elected democratically by the free citizens of each state who, because of their economic situation, had won electoral rights. Compared with the governors, designated by the metropolis, they came to have a strong power. It was based in the fundamental right conceded to each English citizen, the right to representation. Because of this, the Americans thought, they should have in the colonies a function similar to that of Parliament in England, and should enjoy the same prerogatives. Among these they counted the right to establish taxes. When the British Parliament tried to impose taxes on the colonies, it adopted attributes which did not belong to it.

(4) It was the metropolis which had stopped

treating the Americans as free citizens, by attempting to impose upon them the power of a body, the Parliament, in which Americans were not represented. It was the English who violated their own constitution, and betrayed the spirit of their Glorious Revolution, by trying to abolish the liberties which the revolution had conferred. On the other hand, the Americans appealed to this constitution which they considered forgotten and corrupted by the British government. The independence movement did not radically change the society; it claimed, on the contrary, to restore the principles which governed it.

In New Spain the situation was more complex, because together with the thought of that sector of the elite favorable to independence, there appeared another, stimulated by the revolutionary uprising of the lower classes. To avoid confusion at this point, I will limit my discussion to the ideas which became evident in 1808, before the popular uprising, and which culminated in 1821, after the rebellion had been put down.

To establish the equality of the rights of New Spain with those of the metropolis, the creoles were unable to appeal to an immediate antecedent as were North Americans. But the intellectual movement is the same. Since the conquest of America, the creoles maintained, a "pact" had existed between the Americans and the King, confirmed by subsequent laws. According to this pact, it was a question of independent nations, subject to the same sovereign. Spain had, before the King, the same rights and duties as Castile or Leon, and the King must act as if he belonged to each nation. New Spain was not subject to Castile, but only to the Crown. One of the most astute ideologues of this period, Servando Teresa de Mier, coined an expression to designate this original "pact": he spoke of an "American Constitution."

It was the Spaniards who betrayed this ancient "constitution." In reality, the betrayal began with the sixteenth century when the liberties of the people yielded to the absolutism of the kings. Thus, the creoles returned to a past prior to despotism. In Castilian laws of the Middle Ages (the *Leyes de Partida*) they read, for example, that should they be without a monarch, the free men of the villages should meet in assemblies which would maintain custody of the kingdom and govern it. This was what the creoles of New Spain tried to do faced with the pressure of the monarchy. Returning to their own tradition, they remembered the meetings of town councils, and attempted to revive them. In New Spain, in fact, there were no state assemblies similar to those of the North American colonies. But there still lived an organism which traditionally was seen as representative of a popular power against a despotic central government: the *ayuntamiento,* or town council. In the political thought of the creoles, these bodies played a role similar to that of the Lower Houses in the Thirteen Colonies. Like the Lower Houses, the councils were not in reality dominated by the lower classes, but by the "honorable Men" of a certain economic and social position: the property owners and educated who were able to control them. In the councils, civil and ecclesiastic, they saw the power to oppose the viceregal absolutism, and when in the first years of the movement, they spoke of a "congress," the creoles were not referring to a chamber of representatives elected by universal suffrage, but to a meeting of the councils of the towns. In North America as in New Spain, democracy was not understood as direct majority representation of the lower classes, but as the power of free men of a particular social position, represented in bodies which were already constituted.

In both cases we encounter a paradox: the reform movement which fought to break dependence was also a movement to return to the beginnings of the colonial society itself. It was presented as a restoration and defense of the institutions and authentic values against a conspiracy of the absolutism which attempted to destroy them. The Americans, in the North as well as in the South, confronting external impositions, attempted to go back to what was "right," even though this "right" varied in each case. The North Americans felt themselves defenders of the true English liberties and keepers of the spirit of their "Revolution." The Mexicans called themselves the "true Spaniards," branded the Europeans as Francophiles, and demanded the restoration of Spanish laws nullified by despotism. The traditions were distinct, but the historical attitude was the same.

It is not surprising that in the final phase of the two movements for independence we come across notable parallels, since in both cases similar sectors of the colonial elite obtained the victory.

An influential North American historiographical current, the so-called "Progressive" history (Schlesinger, Beard, Jensen, among others) sustained the thesis, accepted for many years, that the North American Constitution of 1787 signified a "counterrevolutionary" movement against the beginnings of independence, as expressed in the Declaration of Independence. The Constitution was the political instrument which the elites adopted to deter the danger of direct popular power. This interpretation has sustained multiple objections and subsequent revisions which prevent us from accepting it fully. Nevertheless, even though we may not subscribe to the thesis that North American independence ended in a counterrevolution, we can accept the argument that the elaboration of the Constitution did signal a certain change of emphasis when compared to the Declaration of Independence. The most recent studies (Hartz, Wright, Baylin, Kenyon, and others) permit us to conclude that even if the independence movement had from its beginnings the intention of preserving the rights existent in the colonies, this "conservative" function was accentuated at the end, in the elaboration of the constitutions. State charters of 1776, 1777, and 1780 emphasized order and stability as much as liberty, and showed special commitment to the defense of the rights of property and individual liberty. In the discussions which led to the promulgation of the Federal Constitution, the "stabilizing" and "preserving" tendency is clear. It was no longer a question of promoting and establishing the direct power of the people, but of mounting the mechanisms which might make possible a strong central government and protecting it against the anarchistic action of the majority. Madison and his followers tried to establish the legal correctives against an uncontrollable popular power. The separation of powers, the bicameral system, and the mechanisms of "checks and balances" which the Constitution established, cannot be seen as anything less than a counterweight to direct popular power. Above all, the establishment of the Senate is considered a conservative power, dominated by the richest property owners, and able to moderate or deter the decisions of the majorities. The conservative character of the Constitution has been emphasized for good reason.

Following the defeat of the popular rebellion in New Spain, independence was achieved in 1821, thanks to a movement headed by a creole oligarchy—clergy, landholders and middle classes. Its object was not to overturn the colonial society, but to preserve it against the liberal measures which at that time had been revived in Spain. It was dominated by the idea that the change would preserve an earlier organic continuity. It was a question of "untying without breaking" the bonds of the past, of maintaining respect through existing powers and institutions. Iturbide and his party sought a way to independence which would close the door to an uncontrollable popular drive for power. Against a proposal for one representative assembly, inspired by the French Revolution, they leaned toward a moderate constitution, resembling the English, and toward establishing a Senate of distinguished men to moderate the actions of the lower chamber.

Thus, despite their differences, both independence movements ended by trying to preserve order and stability in the middle of change, and by establishing counterweights to the power of the majority. Nevertheless, their conservative character has distinct nuances: In the United States, "to conserve" is also to maintain a popular power already existing, though limited; in Mexico, "to conserve" is to sustain a state of social privilege.

III

At this juncture we have been able to identify certain common features in the two independence movements, in the economic condition as well as the mentality of the leading groups. But this parallel crumbles when we consider another element which indicates a radical difference between the two movements: the common people. The introduction of this dissonant factor in the picture we have traced permits us to understand the individuality of each movement.

In the North American colonies a majority of the adult males possessed property sufficient to gain electoral rights. Except for the existence in the South of Negro slaves and a small marginal population, North American society was relatively free from poverty. It was probably the freest society, with the fewest class distinctions, of its time. The intervention of the common people in their own behalf was also rare in the independence movement. Except for the uprisings after the promulgation of the Stamp Act, the lower classes followed the leadership and made common cause with them. Finally, in the constitutional discussions, the anti-federalists were strongly opposed to the constitution of a centralized government and to the attempt to restrain local popular power. But the anti-federalists could not identify with the lower classes. Moreover, as Lee Benson has shown, the anti-federalists were of an "agrarian mentality" (compared to those of a "commercial mentality") who tended to defend their own limited local interests against the intervention of a national state. Furthermore, those groups were never able to put together a force which might seriously endanger the constitution of the new social system.

In New Spain the picture is completely different. Here the elite which favored independence not only had to confront the dominant sector of the oligarchy itself, but also a miserable underclass, dispossessed of almost all their rights.

At the base of the social pyramid, the workers of New Spain, composed of Indians and castes, shared only their extreme misery. The increase in wealth at the end of the eighteenth century had benefitted the economic oligarchy and, at the same time, aggravated social distinctions. Nowhere, said Humboldt, had he seen "such tremendous inequality in the distribution of wealth, of culture, of the cultivation of land, and of people."

In the countryside, the expansion of the haciendas at the expense of the communal Indian lands had increased unemployment and favored the creation of an extensive peonage for the large estates. While the prices of food grains rose continually, the wages of the peons remained constant. Indians and Castes were menaced periodically by the worst scourge: hunger. The great agrarian crisis, in which the scarce corn, hoarded by the landowners, became inaccessible, had as a sequel epidemics of generalized starvation which devastated entire regions. The generation which would achieve independence had lived through one of these disasters, when in 1785 and 1786 the loss of harvests gave rise to innumerable deaths.

In comparison with the rural peons, the workers in the mines, although working under extremely difficult conditions, were better paid. They constituted a force of free, and highly mobile, labor. Nevertheless, their condition had worsened at the end of the century. Indeed, many mine owners began to reduce or suppress the "partidas," that is, the right of the workers to retain part of the ore. The situation of the workers in the factories was probably worse than that of the miners. The workday was not regulated; the workers lacked any special legislation on their behalf; and in many enterprises they were forced to live in the factory like prisoners, subject to rigid discipline.

But the most severe problem at the beginning of the nineteenth century was the disproportionate growth of the urban lower classes. The last decades of the eighteenth century witnessed a notable demographic growth which, combined with increased rural unemployment and the expansion of work in the cities, created an enormous underclass which increased rapidly in the cities, searching uselessly for something to do. The censuses indicate that only a meager portion of the urban population was occupied in productive activity. Humboldt pointed to the existence in Mexico City of at least 30,000 unemployed, ragged and miserable. This lower class was ripe for a violent eruption.

Then, between the first proposals for reform put forth in 1808 by the Ayuntamiento of Mexico City and the achievement of independence in 1821, a violent popular uprising intervened, which pitted the lowest classes against the upper classes. This gives a character of internal class struggle to the independence movement of New Spain. The revolution which broke out in 1810, led by Miguel Hidalgo and subsequently by José María Morelos, was a tumultuous uprising of rural Indians, mine workers, and the urban underclass, incited and directed by a radical group of middle class intellectuals. Opposed to the revolution were not just those sectors openly royalist, but also all of the creole elements of the upper classes, even those which sympathized with independence.

The first proposal for a political constitution grew out of the heart of this movement, and here, too, the Republic was proclaimed. The revolutionary intellectuals who supported the popular movement radicalized their thought on contact with the masses. They proclaimed the equality of the Indians and castes, abolished slavery—the first emancipation in all America—and reclaimed the land for the Indian communities. At first they continued the line of thought which appealed to the Hispanic traditions prior to despotism, but soon they went further: they restored the rights of the Indians vis-a-vis the colonizers, and rejected totally the Hispanic past. They gave up the idea of basing the nation on constituted corporate bodies; their democratic model was no longer the *cabildo* or municipal council. Rather they proposed to build the new nation from the

ground up; that is, a negation of the previous social and
political order. A proposal for a single assembly of
representatives of the people, in the French pattern,
replaced the congress of cabildos. It was a question of
creating, from the original "state of nature," a new State,
rationally planned.

This popular revolution failed. After 1814 it could be
considered definitely defeated. From that point, until a
century later, the lower class would not lift its head.
Independence did not bring about a popular rebellion, but
rather a counterrevolutionary movement. Yet, the aborted
revolution left a mark on the thought of the radical sector of
the middle class which adhered to it and stamped with its
seal all of nineteenth century Mexical liberalism. This radical
group abandoned the notion that any real achievement of
popular power would be gained other than through a
movement of conversion: through the negation of the
existing order and a reconstitution of the nation beginning
with free and direct elections by the people. The model
could no longer be a royalist constitution, adapted to
tradition, which preserved an existing social status, but one
which rose from a rational outline designing a new social
order. From then on the rationalist—and often utopian—
character of liberalism developed. The subsequent struggle
for liberty in Mexico found its point of departure in this
popular movement which failed, and not in the achievement
of independence. And this is where the parallel with the
history of the United States is broken and where we open
for ourselves a path to better understanding the particulars
of the subsequent histories of each of these peoples.

IV

We have arrived at the point of restating several conclusions:

(1) In the colonies of the North as in New Spain, independence occurred at a time of economic growth which was hindered by the policy of the metropolis, which was attempting to reinforce a situation of dependence and exploitation. In both cases the principal obstruction was located in the legislative and political order. The movement had a sense of joining this order to royal encroachment on civil society.

(2) The structure of dependence was, however, different in each case. The economic base of New Spain was an "enclave" economy, which was not the case in North America. Because of this, the movement in New Spain revealed the division in the upper classes. If in the Thirteen Colonies this division was less pronounced, it was because of its distinct economic situation.

(3) In both cases sectors of the colonial elite began and ended the movement. From this stemmed its ambiguous character: independence was at the same time a reformist and a conservative movement. It tried to break political and economic dependence while preserving the social structure of the old colony. In the intellectual sphere, it was expressed in a movement to return to the origins of the colony and restore its own liberal tradition. In both movements, the achievement of independence was seen as a legitimization of bodies of power already existent in the colony: the lower houses, the town councils. Because of this, in neither of the two countries did independence end the struggle with a government directly of the people; it merely marked a beginning.

(4) Against this common general framework, the divergences which give each movement its own character stand out. In the United States independence did little more, as Bernard Bailyn has said, than "complete, formalize, systematize, and symbolize," an order based on liberty. To realize democracy, it did not seem necessary to overturn the social order, but only to reaffirm and generalize an existing popular power. The liberal order did not stem from a negation of the past, but from a continuation with it. As Hannah Arendt astutely observed, the North American revolution did not plan a return to a "state of nature" (to use the language of the Enlightenment), because the people in the colonies were already organized in democratic organisms. Independence consisted, therefore, in the elimination of obstacles which opposed the exercise of this democratic power. It did not consist in the negation of a social system and the election of a new one, but in "a movement to restore and recover old laws and liberties." The North American nation was not born under the sign of social revolution, but of constitutional democracy.

In New Spain, on the contrary, the liberal constitution did not coincide with independence. It is the result of a movement of radical rejection of the past and of the rational choice of a different state of affairs. It expresses the destructive and liberating action of popular uprising. Because the power of the people had to be *created*, liberty had to be established through revolution. The Mexican nation was not born under the sign of constitutional democracy, but of a frustrated and delayed social revolution.

Perhaps this profound divergence, which presided over the birth of each nation, allows us to better understand how, in their common pursuit of liberty, these countries arrived at their diverse points of view. The United States began its life with the restoration of democracy, and at the same time, with the establishment of systems which limited it. The majority of North Americans has tended to view the final realization of liberty, not in a revolutionary movement which might call into question the social structure, but rather in complete fulfillment of the democratic credo on which the nation is founded, and in the elimination of everything opposed to its full completion. They understand with difficulty that for Mexicans, not political democracy, but social revolution is the authentic way to achieve liberty. Far from seeing in revolution a movement which leads to liberty, they consider it a menace to democracy.

Mexico, on the other hand, initiated its independent life after the failure of a popular libertarian movement. Liberty is not identified with the treaties which seal its independence, but as an interrupted project for the negation of the existing society. The majority of Mexicans, therefore, is accustomed to see the realization of a social revolution, frequently attempted and always thwarted, as the only way to gain the establishment of liberty. They do not generally understand how many North Americans can claim to defend democracy while they are at the same time opposing popular revolutionary movements. Because, in our history, political democracy is not identified with liberty. And the magic halo which the word "democracy" possesses in the United States, in Mexico has been acquired by another word, "revolution."

2

The Forgotten Experience: Indians, Blacks and the American Revolution

Gary B. Nash

I N APRIL 1787, a month before the Constitutional Convention met in Philadelphia to draw up the culminating document of the revolutionary era, a man whom nobody commemorated in the Bicentennial year, sent these words to a friend: "If I fall by the hand of such [assassins], I shall fall a victim in the noblest of causes—that of falling in maintaining the just rights of my country. I aspire to the honest ambition of meriting the appelation of preserver of my country, equally with those chiefs among you, whom from acting on such principles, you have exalted to the highest pitch of glory; and if, after every peaceable mode of obtaining a redress of grievances having proved fruitless, the having recourse to arms to obtain it, be marks of the savage, and not of the soldier, what savages must the Americans be...."[1] The author of those words was Hoboi-Hili-Miko, a leader of the Creek Indians of the lower South and known in white communities of Georgia and South Carolina as Alexander McGillivray, after his father, a Scotch-Irish immigrant who had come to America about 1738, had taken up life as an Indian trader in South Carolina, and married a Creek woman.

McGillivray's remark was made at a time when the government of Georgia had a contract on his life because of the fierce resistance he was leading to encroaching white frontiersmen, who coveted the rich lands on which the Creek people had dwelt for centuries.[2] His words serve as a reminder that the American Revolution was more than a struggle between highly principled American colonists and a tyrannical, corrupt mother country. It was more even than a war of national liberation overlaid by an internal struggle among patriots concerning the kind of society that should emerge if the war was won. Seen most broadly, the Revolution was an era of social upheaval and military conflict in which a bewildering variety of people were swept into a whirlpool of ideas and events, forced to decide what it was they believed in, and obligated—as happens to few of us in the modern age—to risk everything in defense of those beliefs. Some of these people were white, some were black, and some were red. McGillivray of the Creeks was red; and like so many of the heroes commemorated in the

Bicentennial year, he decided that what he believed in was the preservation of political liberty for his people, the maintenance of their cultural integrity, and the safeguarding of the land that their ancestors had inhabited from time out of mind.[3]

What has been largely lost in our recording of American history—and what was systematically excluded from the portrayal of the Revolution on television in 1976— is the fact that for many of the people of North America the struggle for life, liberty, and the pursuit of happiness in the 1770s and 1780s was carried on by fighting with the British and against those American minutemen and other anti-British patriots upon whom our patriotic celebrations have always exclusively focused. The story of these "other" patriots deserves our attention too, if we mean to honor, two hundred years after the fact, *all* those who struggled for freedom, justice, and opportunity.

Take, for example, Thomas Peters. In 1759, the year of Alexander McGillivray's birth and—*annus mirabilus*—the year that the British and their colonial partners drove the French from the Plains of Abraham at Quebec, thus ending French pretensions in North America, Peters had never heard of the thirteen American colonies. For he was an Egba of the Yoruba tribe, living in what is now Nigera and known, of course, by a different name. But a year later he was in the New World. Kidnapped by slave traders, carried across the Atlantic, sold at auction in French Louisiana, Peters lost not only his Egba name but also his liberty, his dreams of happiness, and very nearly his life. Shortly thereafter, he started his own revolution in America because he had been deprived of what he considered, without benefit of a written language or constitutional treatises, as his natural rights. Three times he tried to escape another human being who called him chattel property, thus proclaiming, within the context of his own experience, that all men are created equal. Three times he paid the price of unsuccessful black revolutionaries—first whippings, then branding, and finally ankle shackles.[4]

By the early 1770s Peters had been sold to a plantation owner in Wilmington, North Carolina, perhaps because his former master had wearied of trying to snuff out the yearning for freedom that seemed to beat irrepressibly in his breast. On the eve of the Revolution, then in his 30s and well acculturated to the ways of the New World slave colonies, Peters struck his next blow for freedom. Pamphleteers all over the colonies were crying out against British oppression, British tyranny, British plans to enslave the Americans. But in Norfolk, Virginia, about two hundred miles from his owner's plantation, the royal governor of Virginia, Lord Dunmore, in November 1775, proclaimed life-long freedom to any American slave or indentured servant "able and willing to bear arms" who escaped his freedom-loving master and made it to the British lines.[5] Peters broke the law of North Carolina, redefined himself as man instead of property, and made good his escape. For the rest of the war he fought in the British Regiment of Black Guides and Pioneers. Twice wounded and promoted to sergeant, he made a wartime marriage to another black freedom fighter, a slave woman who had escaped her master in Charleston, South Carolina about the time the colonial delegates to the Second Continental Congress were gathering in Philadelphia to sign the great document by which they collectively emancipated themselves from their master.

At the end of the war, Peters, his wife, and hundreds of other members of the Black Guides and Pioneers were evacuated from New York City to Nova Scotia by the

British.[6] There could be no staying in the land of the victorious American revolutionaries, for only Vermont among the territories of the new republic had ended slavery,[7] and those who had fought with the British were particularly hated and subject to retaliation. To remain in America meant running the risk of re-enslavement.[8] Moreover, the British promised land, tools, and rations for three years to those who had fought alongside them against the rebellious colonists. But in Nova Scotia the dream of life, liberty, and happiness turned into a nightmare. Some 3,000 ex-slaves found that they were segregated in impoverished villages, given small scraps of often untillable land, deprived of rights normally extended to British subjects, and reduced to peonage by a white population whose racism was as congealed as the frozen winter soil of Nova Scotia.[9] White Nova Scotians were no more willing than Americans to accept blacks as better than slaves, as was made abundantly clear less than a year after Peters and his people arrived from New York. Hundreds of disbanded British soldiers, who were taking up settlement in Nova Scotia, attacked black villages, burned and looted, and pulled down the houses of free blacks who underbid their labor in the area.[10]

After several years of frustration, Peters determined to journey to England to put the case of the black Nova Scotians before the British government. He sailed in July 1791, and in London met with leaders of the English abolitionist movement—Granville Sharp, Thomas Clarkson, and William Wilburforce—men who were already working to establish a free black colony on the west coast of Africa, especially for ex-slaves, many of them refugees from America, living in poverty in London. By 1792 the plan was perfected. The colony was to be called Sierra Leone and its capital city would be Freetown. Peters returned to Nova

Scotia, accompanied by John Clarkson, the younger brother of Thomas; spread the word of a return to the homeland; and played a galvanizing role in organizing the pilgrimage back to the part of the world from whence many of his compatriots had started half a lifetime before.[11] In January 1792, fifteen ships with some 1,200 black Canadians weighed anchor, set their sails to the east, and followed this Black Moses away from the New World. Legend tells that Peters, sick from shipboard fever, led his people ashore in Sierra Leone singing, "The Day of jubilee is come, return ye ransomed sinners home." Four months later he was dead.[12]

Peters deserves a prominent place in any commemoration of the American Revolution that pays heed to the principles upon which the American struggle was based, for he waged an epic, half-century struggle for the most basic political rights, for social equity, and for human dignity. For Peters, as for almost all Afro-Americans in the 1770s, this struggle involved a reckoning of which side of the family quarrel to take in order to pursue their personal freedom as opposed to the nation's freedom. As Benjamin Quarles has said, the "major loyalty [of black revolutionaries] was not to a place nor a people but to a principle."[13] If the principle could best be achieved by joining the British, then why should it matter whether the king and parliament were taxing the Americans without representation or quartering troops in Boston? Such infringements of white rights paled by comparison to the violation of black rights by these same Americans, as even some white revolutionaries admitted. If, on the other hand, the British army was nowhere near, then service on the American side might earn a slave his freedom.

So black Americans made their choices according to the circumstances in which they found themselves. In many of the colonies they were quick to petition the legislatures for their freedom even before the fighting broke out and they were helped along by scores of white revolutionaries, who like the clergyman Samuel Hopkins of Connecticut, called for "universal liberty to white and black" and pointed out "the shocking, the intolerable, the ... gross barefaced practiced inconsistence" of the patriots inveighing against the slavery imposed by king and parliament on the colonies while at the same time they consigned to "unutterable wretchedness" many thousands of poor blacks "who have as good a claim to liberty as themselves."[14] But black Americans quickly learned in the early years of the war that the chances for a general emancipation were almost nil. Many white patriots, North and South, believed that slavery was a grotesque contradiction of the revolutionary credo. But they regarded the social and economic costs of emancipation as too high a price to pay. Thus blacks learned not to look to white society for their liberty, but to seize the moment, whenever and wherever it presented itself, to liberate themselves.

It is not surprising, then, that in almost every part of the colonies black Americans took advantage of wartime disruption to obtain their freedom in any way they could. Sometimes they joined the American army, often serving in place of their masters who gladly gave black men freedom in order not to risk life and limb for the cause. Sometimes they served with their masters on the battlefield as orderlies and hoped for the rewards of freedom at war's end. Such was the case of William Lee, Washington's slave, who appears at the General's side in many paintings of the period but had to wait until Washington's death in 1799 to collect his reward. Sometimes black Americans served with such heroism that white society gladly gave freedom for services rendered, as in the case of James Armistead, who enlisted under General Lafayette in 1781, infiltrated Cornwallis's camp at Yorktown, providing valuable information for the revolutionary army, and lived, a free man after the war, to greet the French general when he returned to America in 1824 to visit his friend, Thomas Jefferson.[15] Sometimes Afro-Americans tried to burst the shackles of slavery by fleeing all the white combatants and seeking refuge among the trans-Allegheny Indian tribes. But most frequently freedom was sought by joining the British whenever their regiments were close enough to reach.[16] Acting very little like the dependent, childlike Sambos that some historians have described, black Americans took up arms, so far as we can tell, in as great a proportion to their numbers as did white Americans.[17] Well they might, for while white revolutionaries were fighting to protect liberties long enjoyed, black revolutionaries were fighting to gain liberties long denied. Even in the areas where slavery was practiced in its mildest forms, such as in Quaker Philadelphia, slaves made their bid for freedom. When the British occupied the city in late 1777, slaves fled their masters by the scores. "The defection of the Negroes," wrote one Philadelphian, "even of the most indulgent masters... shows what little dependence ought to be placed on persons deprived of their natural rights."[18]

We could draw up a roster of black revolutionary heroes as long as the time-honored list of whites: Agrippa Hull, the free black who served two years in the Massachusetts line and four years more as orderly for the Polish patriot general, Tadeusz Kosciusko; John Marrant, the black evangelist who lived and preached among the Cherokees in the early 1770s, fought with the British during the war, ministered among the relocated blacks of Nova

Scotia in the 1780s, and returned to American soil in the 1790s to become the chaplain in Boston of the first American Black Masonic Lodge; David George, founder of the first black Baptist church, gathered among slaves at Silver Bluff, South Carolina in 1773; and Richard Allen, a founder of the Free African Society in Philadelphia in 1787—the first black organization for social and economic cooperation in America—and co-founder of the first free black church in Pennsylvania.[19] But while it is important to recall these black leaders, it also needs to be recognized that at a very common level, within the slave quarters of thousands of southern plantations and in the kitchens and backrooms of thousands of northern farms, ordinary black Americans were deciding that the moment had come when they must say, "Give me liberty or give me death."

Perhaps only 20 percent or less of the American slaves gained their freedom and survived the war—and many of them faced years of travail and even re-enslavement thereafter in Nova Scotia, England, the West Indies, and British Florida. But their story is an extraordinarily important part of a tradition of black protest and struggle that did not die with the Peace of Paris in 1783. The American Revolution was the first large-scale rebellion of American slaves, and we must link their quest with the struggles of nineteenth-century black abolitionists and resistant slaves who drew inspiration from their work. It was a rebellion, to be sure, that was carried on individually rather than collectively for the most part because circumstances favored individualized struggles for freedom. But out of thousands of individualized acts grew a legend of black strength, black vision for the future, black resistance to slavery and institutionalized white racism. Personified in the lifelong struggle of Thomas Peters, this new determination reemerged after the war, surfacing in the first successful efforts to build black institutions in America, including black schools and fraternal societies in the North and the African Baptist and Methodist-Episcopal churches under sons of the revolution such as David George, Andrew Bryan, Peter Williams, and Absalom Jones. "We are determined to seek out for ourselves," wrote Richard Allen of Philadelphia, "the Lord being our helper."[20]

In the closing decades of the eighteenth century, among both free and slave Afro-Americans, this spirit could not be stifled. The task of a generation of black leaders, who for the most part had seized the opportunities inherent in wartime disruption to gain their own freedom and carve out their own destinies, was to lay the foundations of modern Afro-American culture. Their task was even more formidable because white society after the war abandoned the anti-slavery impulse of the early revolutionary years and entered an era of intensified prejudice against black Americans. By the early nineteenth century the movement to hobble all attempts of the growing free black population to obtain political, social, and economic rights accorded to white citizens was fully underway.[21]

●   ●   ●

For some 200,000 native Americans living between the Atlantic Ocean and the Mississippi River the American Revolution was also a time to "try men's souls." Thayendanegea, known in the English communities as Joseph Brant, stands as an illuminating example. Thayendanegea was a Mohawk, born about the same time as Thomas Peters but in an Iroquois village on the other side of the world. His sister married the prominent William Johnson, who had come to the American colonies in the same year as Alexander

McGillivray's father and quickly became a baronial landowner in New York, the King's Superintendent of Indian Affairs for the northern colonies, and an honorary member of the Mohawk tribe. Thayendanegea spoke English fluently, for he had been educated in Eleazar Wheelock's Indian School in Connecticut, later to become Dartmouth College. He had translated part of the Bible into Mohawk, at age 13 served the Anglo-American cause by fighting with William Johnson against the French at Crown Point in 1755, and four years later aided the colonists again by battling against Pontiac's Indian insurgents, who were determined in the wake of the defeat of the French during the Seven Years' War, to expel the British soldiers and their encroaching American cousins from the Ohio country. Thayendanegea was a man who lived in two worlds—red and white. Bilingual and bicultural, he gravitated between the two.[22]

As he matured in the 1760s, Thayendanegea grew to understand that despite the trading alliance the Iroquois had maintained with the English colonies for generations, and despite the close ties that the Mohawks (the easternmost of the six Iroquois nations) maintained with William Johnson, his people were now seriously threatened by the rapidly growing white population. Barely 20,000 white colonists inhabited New York in 1700, but by 1740 their number had swelled to 65,000 and by 1770 to 160,000. Many times in the twilight of the colonial period the Mohawks had been swindled out of land by rapacious New York land speculators and frontiersmen.[23] So as the war clouds gathered in 1775, Thayendanegea, 33 years old, took ship to London to see what the English king would offer the Iroquois for their support in a war that while still not formally declared had been in the shooting stage since early in the year. Like his grandfather, Chief Hendrick, who had been among the

Iroquois chiefs who travelled to London to consult with
Queen Anne 65 years before, Thayendanegea was greeted as
royalty in England.[24] He was feted by the king, written
about in the *London Universal Magazine*, and had his
portrait painted by Romney. But his mission was to
determine how life, liberty, and the protection of property
might best be preserved by his people. His decision, made
before leaving London, augured the reckoning of a vast
majority of Indian tribes in the next few years—that only by
fighting against the independence-seeking Americans could
Indian tribes themselves remain independent. He returned to
New York a few weeks after the Declaration of
Independence had been signed at Philadelphia, served with
the British General George Howe at Long Island in the first
major defeat of Washington's army, and then in November
1776 began a long trek through the lands of the Iroquois and
their confederates in the Ohio country to spread the
message, as he wrote, that "their own Country and Liberty"
were "in danger from the Rebels."[25] Thayendanegea's
diplomatic mission was crucial in bringing most of the
Iroquois into the war on the British side in the summer of
1777.

   During the war Thayendanegea was everywhere—at
Oriskany in August 1777 when the British and their Indian
allies, in perhaps the bloodiest battle of the revolution,
defeated the Americans who were trying to reach the
besieged Fort Stanwix, which controlled access to the
western Mohawk Valley and the Greak Lakes; at Cherry
Valley in the summer of 1778, when the Iroquois drove
thousands of American farmers from their fields in southern
New York and northern Pennsylvania; and at a dozen battles
in the campaign of 1779 when the American General John
Sullivan invaded the Iroquois country, burning towns and

scorching the earth. For the entire war, Thayendanegea played a leading role in virtually eliminating the New York and Pennsylvania back-country, a major grain and cattle-growing area upon which the Continental army had depended for supplies, from contributing much to the war effort. "A thousand Iroquois warriors and five hundred Tory rangers," writes one historian, "were able to lay in waste nearly 50,000 square miles of colonial territory."[26]

Though never militarily defeated during the war, the Iroquois were abandoned by their British allies at the peace talks in Paris and left in 1783 to cope with a highly militarized and land-hungry American people. Confronting insurmountable odds, the Iroquois signed dictated treaties that dispossessed them of most of their land and consigned them to reservations that within a generation became "slums in the wilderness." Thayendanegea spent the last twenty years of his life trying to lead the Iroquois in adjusting to the harsh new realities by which a proud and independent people found that the pursuit of happiness by white Americans required red Americans to surrender life, liberty, and property.[27]

The story of Thayendanegea and the Iroquois encapsulates important facets of the Indians' American Revolution. At the heart of this red struggle were the twin goals of political independence and territorial defense. Black Americans, who had neither liberty nor land, fought for the former in order someday to gain the latter. Red Americans, who had both, struggled to preserve both. Like most black Americans, almost all Indian tribes concluded that their revolutionary goals could best be achieved through fighting *against* the side that proclaimed the equality of all men and with the side that the Americans accused of trampling on their natural, irreducible rights. The logic of nearly two hundred years of abrasive contact with colonizing Europeans compelled the choice, for it was the settler-subjects of the English king who most threatened Indian autonomy, just as it was the royal power that before the Revolution had attempted to protect Indian land from white encroachment by means of the Proclamation Line of 1763 and the regulation of trade.[28]

In pursuing their revolutionary goals, Indian tribes shared with the American enemy the problem of how to overcome a long tradition of local identity and inter-tribal factionalism—how, in other words, to forge a confederated resistance movement. Just as the white "tribes" of Connecticut and New York had to put aside localist attachments and longstanding disagreements, just as Virginians and North Carolinians had to bury animosities that went back several generations, just as northern and southern colonies had to compose their differences, so the Iroquois, Shawnee, Cherokee, Delaware, Creek, Miami, and other tribes searched for ways to forge a pan-Indian movement out of generations of inter-tribal suspicion or conflict. For the white revolutionists, as John Adams said, the issue was to make thirteen clocks strike as one. For the red revolutionists east of the Mississippi the problem was identical. In both societies new leaders emerged in the process of wrestling with this central question, and usually they were men whose military abilities or political persuasiveness gained them attention, suggesting that the fate of their people lay in their hands. Our history books rarely record the names of Red Jacket or Cornplanter of the Seneca, Attakullakulla and Dragging Canoe of the Cherokees, Red Shoes of the Creek, White Eyes of the Delaware, or Little Turtle of the Miami; but they were as much the dominant new figures of the revolutionary era in Indian society as were Washington,

Hamilton, Nathaniel Greene, Richard Henry Lee, and John Paul Jones in white society. Moreover, they were well known to the revolutionary leaders, for the Indian tribes of the interior were formidable adversaries who could never be ignored.

In the end, the Indians were disastrously the losers in the war of the American Revolution. Partly this was because they were less successful than the thirteen white tribes in overcoming inter-tribal factionalism; partly it was because the supplies of European trade goods upon which they depended — especially guns, powder, and shot — were seriously disrupted during the war; and partly it was because they were abandoned to the Americans by their British allies at war's end. Facing a white society in 1783 that was heavily armed and obsessed with the vision of western lands, tribes such as the Iroquois and Cherokee were forced to cede away most of their land. The pre-war white population buildup, which had caused worsening economic conditions in many older communities along the coastal plain, was relieved as thousands of white Americans spilled across the mountains after 1783, frequently in violation of treaties contracted by their own elected governments. Aiding these frontiersmen, many of them war veterans, were state and national governments, which understood that the western lands, once the native inhabitants had been driven away, were the new nation's most valuable resource. The sale of western lands would provide the revenue both to liquidate the huge war debt and to underwrite the expenses of a nation of tax-shy people.[29]

Such a policy required the newly independent American republic systematically to sacrifice the sanctity of its own laws and treaty obligations and to abandon the revolutionary ideal of just and equitable relations among men. Some white leaders were troubled by this, such as George Morgan, a former Indian trader and agent for the Continental Congress, who wrote in 1793: "At what time do a People violate the Law of Nations, as the U[nited] S[tates] have done, with regard to the N[orth] W[estern] Indians? Only when they think they can do it with Impunity. Justice between Nations is founded on reciprocal Fear. Rome whilst weak was equitable; become more strong than her Neighbors, she ceased to be just. The ambitious & powerful are always unjust. To them the Laws of Nations are mere Chimeras."[30] But most Americans were no more willing to apply the principles emblazoned on the revolutionary banners to relations with the Indian inhabitants of the trans-Allegheny region than they were to fulfill the revolutionary ideal of abolishing slavery. Indian land, like black slave labor, was one of the new republic's pre-eminently important resources. To forego its exploitation was beyond the collective will of a people whose colonial background had inculcated the ideal of individualistic, material aggrandizement alongside the ideals of political freedom and religious liberty.

In the last analysis, the pro-British stance of the Native Americans cannot be accounted a failure of judgment on their part. Had they sided with the Americans they would have fared no better, as the dismal post-war experience of several pro-American tribes such as the Tuscaroras and Oneidas demonstrates. Moreover, the wartime attempts at inter-tribal confederation played a large role in mounting the next great Indian resistance movement, from about 1783 to 1815, when white Americans, having won a war of national liberation, embarked on a war of national expansion.[31] Thayendanegea's wartime exertions and his efforts, after another trip to London in 1785, to foster inter-tribal cooperation, led to fierce Indian resistance in the Old Northwest. Similarly, in the Old Southwest, Alexander McGillivray was galvanizing Creek resistance to land-hungry South Carolinans and Georgians. "Our lands are our life and breath," he wrote; "if we part with them, we part with our blood. We must fight for them."[32]

Thayendanegea and McGillivray were the exemplars of pan-Indian resistance. From the work of a host of such war-tempered Indian leaders arose a new generation of resistance leaders—Black Hawk, Tecumeseh, and others. The tribes of the Ohio Valley fought desperately in the post-war era to protect their homelands, only to lose against overwhelming odds when state militias and federal armies, whom they had defeated in the late 1780s and early 1790s, came back with larger and larger forces to invade their land. By this time the humanitarian language of the Northwest Ordinance of 1787 had been all but forgotten. "The utmost good faith," promised the Continental Congress in its last significant act, "shall always be observed towards the Indians; their lands and property shall never be taken from them without their consent; and in their property, rights and liberty, they never shall be invaded or disturbed, unless in just and lawful wars authorized by Congress; but laws founded in justice and humanity shall from time to time be made, for preventing wrongs being done to them, and for preserving peace and friendship with them."[33] As the strengthening of state militias and the creation of a national army progressed in the 1790s, Indian societies learned how hollow were the phrases of the Northwest Ordinance. Armed conflict replaced "utmost good faith" with the republic's greatest revolutionary hero, now its first president, capturing the national mood when he wrote: "The gradual extension of our settlements will as certainly cause the Savage as the

Wolf to retire; both being beasts of prey tho' they differ in shape."[34]

•   •   •

In looking backward on the 200th birthday of our nation we need to broaden our perspective so as to recognize that the revolution—fought by white Americans for life, liberty, and the pursuit of happiness—compelled many non-white Americans to take the other side in quest of the same goals. The red and black people of this land were animated by the doctrine of natural rights as surely as were the minutemen at Concord Bridge or the signers of the Declaration of Independence; and they were as moved by self-interest as were white revolutionaries. Most of them took the other side to gain or preserve these rights and to pursue their own interests, which had been defined by generations of interaction among red, white, and black people in America. In their struggle against the white revolutionaries most of them lost, at least in the proximate sense. What they won, however, was a piece of history, for they kept lit the lamp of liberty and passed on their own revolutionary heritage to their children and their children's children. The founding principles of the American Revolution lived on in the nineteenth-century struggles of Denmark Vesey, Nat Turner, Frederick Douglas, Black Hawk, Tecumseh, Sequoyah, and a host of other black and red leaders. They live on yet today, for what we proudly call the Spirit of '76 in our white-oriented history books has been at the ideological core of the Black Protest Movement of the 1960s and the Indian Rights Movement of the 1970s. In this sense, the American Revolution, in the year of the Bicentennial, is far from over.

NOTES

1. McGillivray to James White [Superintendent of Indian Affairs for the United States], April 8, 1787, *American State Papers, Indian Affairs* (Washington, 1832), VII, 18. Also see McGillivray to Arturo O'Neill, March 4 and April 18, 1787, in John Walton Caughey, *McGillivray of the Creeks* (Norman, Okla., 1938), pp. 144, 149.

2. For the background of Creek-American relations see David Corkran, *The Creek Frontier, 1540-1783* (Norman, Okla., 1967); Randolph C. Downes, "Creek-American Relations, 1782-1790," *Georgia Historical Quarterly*, 21 (1937), 142-84, and John W. Caughey, "Alexander McGillivray and the Creek Crisis, 1783-1784," *New Spain and the Anglo-American West; Historical Contributions Presented to Herbert Eugene Bolton* (2 vols.; Los Angeles, 1932) I, 263-88.

3. The remarkable career of McGillivray has gone almost unnoticed in the Bicentennial year. As early as 1851 one of the foremost nineteenth-century historians of the South, Albert J. Pickett, wrote: "We doubt if Alabama has ever produced, or ever will produce, a man of greater ability... We have called him the Talleyrand of Alabama." *History of Alabama and Incidentally of Georgia and Mississippi* (2 vols.; Charleston, 1851), quoted in Caughey, *McGillivray of the Creeks*, p. 34. In addition to the references in notes 1 and 2 useful material on McGillivray can be found in Arthur P. Whitaker, "Alexander McGillivray," *North Carolina Historical Review*, 5 (1928), 181-203, 289-309; Carolyn T. Foreman, "Alexander McGillivray, Emperor of the Creeks," *Chronicles of Oklahoma*, 11 (1929), 106-19; and James H. O'Donnell, "Alexander McGillivray; Training for Leadership, 1777-1783," *Georgia Historical Quarterly*, 49 (1965), 172-86.

4. The details of Peters's life will probably always be fragmentary, especially for the years before 1776 when he begins to appear in the British military records. The best sketches of his life are in Sidney Kaplan, *The Black Presence in the Era of the American Revolution, 1770-1800* (New York, 1973), pp. 68-71; and

C.H. Fyfe, "Thomas Peters: History and Legend," *Sierra Leone Studies*, New Series, I [1953], 4, 11. Much valuable detail can also be found in Robin W. Winks, *The Blacks in Canada; A History* (New Haven, 1971).

5. For Dunmore's proclamation see Benjamin Quarles, *The Negro in the American Revolution* (Chapel Hill, N.C., 1961), pp. 19-32.

6. *Ibid.*, pp. 158-81.

7. Vermont had petitioned the Continental Congress for status as the fourteenth state but did not achieve recognition of her separation from New York until 1791. In 1777 delegates from eastern New York were elected to draw up a constitution, which was modelled closely on the radical Pennsylvania constitution of the previous year but included a clause abolishing slavery. See Arthur Zilversmit, *The First Emancipation; The Abolition of Slavery in the North* (Chicago, 1967), p. 116.

8. Hundreds of slaves who ran away during the war were able to elude their masters, migrate to distant places, and take up life as free Negroes. Some of those who joined the British army also probably drifted off in this fashion. See Ira Berlin, "The Revolution in Black Life," in Alfred F. Young, ed., *The American Revolution; Essays in the History of American Radicalism* (DeKalb, Ill., 1976), p. 355.

9. Free black Loyalists in Nova Scotia were systematically denied the franchise, service, and the right to trial. James W. St. G. Walker, "Blacks as American Loyalists; The Slaves' War of Independence," *Historical Reflections/Réflexions Historiques*, 2 (1975), 65.

10. The Nova Scotian experience is best chronicled in Winks, *Blacks in Canada*, ch. 2-3; and John N. Grant, "Black Immigrants into Nova Scotia, 1776-1815," *Journal of Negro History*, 58 (1973), 253-70. A forthcoming comprehensive treatment of the subject is James W. St. G. Walker, *The Black Loyalists; The Search for a Promised Land in Nova Scotia and Sierra Leone, 1783-1870* (New York, 1976). For the story of one black Loyalist evacuated from New York City to Nova Scotia in 1783 see Phyllis R. Blakely,

"Boston King; A Negro Loyalist Who Sought Refuge in Nova Scotia," *Dalhousie Review*, 48 (1968-69), 347-56.

11.   Winks, *Blacks in Canada*, pp. 61-72; Mary Beth Norton, "The Fate of Some Black Loyalists of the American Revolution," *Journal of Negro History*, 58 (1973), 402-26.

12.   Christopher Fyfe, *A History of Sierra Leone* (London, 1962), pp. 33-37; Winks, *Blacks in Canada*, pp. 72-78.

13.   Quarles, *The Negro in the American Revolution*, p. 50.

14.   Excellent treatments of the growing anti-slavery sentiment in the years leading up to the Revolution can be found in Winthrop D. Jordan, *White Over Black; American Attitudes Toward the Negro, 1550-1812* (Chapel Hill, N.C., 1968), pp. 269-311; and David Brion Davis, *The Problem of Slavery in Western Culture* (Ithaca, N.Y., 1966), ch. 10-15. The quotation is from Samuel Hopkins, *A Dialogue Concerning the Slavery of Africans...* (Norwich, Conn., 1776), quoted in Bernard Bailyn *The Ideological Origins of the American Revolution* (Cambridge, Mass., 1967), p. 244.

15.   Many of the accounts of blacks who fought with the Americans were set down in the mid-nineteenth century by William C. Nell, *The Colored Patriots of the American Revolution* (Boston, 1855). The emphasis on the wartime experience of a minority of black Americans lasted more than a century. Such historical astigmatism can be largely accounted for by the long struggle of black and white historians to aid the movement for Negro equality in American society. Harriett Beecher Stowe and Wendell Phillips both wrote introductions to Nell's mid-nineteenth century book, making no bones about the fact that it was being published as an abolitionist proof that blacks had always contributed heroically to the building of the American nation.

16.   For a valuable corrective to the tendency of American historians to emphasize the black Americans who fought on the patriot side while ignoring the far larger number of blacks who joined the British see Walker, "Blacks as American Loyalists; The Slaves' War for Independence," *Historical Reflections/ Reflexions Historiques*, 2 (1975), 51-67.

17. Quarles, *Negro in the American Revolution*, is the best treatment of the various strategies for black self-emancipation during the war. For the manumission of blacks by whites see Zilversmit, *The First Emancipation* for the North and Robert McColley, *Slavery and Jeffersonian Virginia* (Urbana, Ill., 1964) for the South. No systematic attempt has yet been made to estimate the number of slaves who fled during the war. See Walker, "Blacks as American Loyalists," p. 55n for a discussion of various estimates. But when the British mounted their southern campaign in 1779 and promised *all* escaped slaves their freedom (instead of only those capable of bearing arms), tens of thousands of slaves flocked to their lines. David Ramsey, the most knowledgeable eighteenth-century historian of South Carolina, thought that at least 25,000 slaves, or about one-third of those in the colony in 1770, were lost during the war. Georgia, according to modern scholars, lost about three-quarters of her 15,000 slaves. In Virginia, by far the largest slaveowning colony, 30,000 slaves ran away in 1778 alone according to Jefferson and probably twice that many, or about 30 percent of the slave population, during the decade beginning in 1775. See John Hope Franklin, *From Slavery to Freedom; A History of Negro Americans* (4th ed., New York, 1974), p. 92.

18. *Pennsylvania Packet*, January 1, 1780. The comment was made during the debate of the state legislature on a bill for abolishing slavery.

19. Kaplan, *Negro Presence in the Era of the American Revolution* is a fine introduction to the lives of many of these revolutionary black leaders. For the collective black experience the essay by Berlin, "The Revolution in Black Life," in Young, *The American Revolution*, is a valuable beginning, although much remains to be done, especially on slave life in the late eighteenth century. For free blacks much can be learned from Berlin's *Slaves Without Masters; The Free Negro in the Antebellum South* (New York, 1974), and Carol V. R. George, *Segregated Sabbaths; Richard Allen and the Rise of Independent Black Churches, 1760-1840* (New York, 1973). The rich possibilities for studying slave life in this period are made manifest in Herbert G. Gutman, *The Black Family in Slavery and Freedom, 1750-1925* (New York, 1975); Eugene D. Genovese, *Roll, Jordan, Roll; The World the Slaves Made* (New York, 1974), and Lawrence W. Levine, *Black Culture*

and Black Consciousness; Afro-American Folk Thought from Slavery to Freedom (New York, 1977).

20.   Kaplan, *Negro Presence*, p. 85.

21.   Leon F. Litwack, *North of Slavery; The Negro in the Free States, 1790-1860* (Chicago, 1961) is the best account of the rapid growth of institutionalized racism in the North. Also see Jordan, *White Over Black*, ch. 11-15; and David Brion Davis, *The Problem of Slavery in the Age of Revolution, 1770-1823* (Ithaca, N.Y., 1975), ch. 6-7. For the extraordinary life of one free northern black, whose identification with his African roots became stronger and stronger in the early nineteenth century, leading him finally into a close association with the recolonization of black Americans to Sierra Leone, see Sheldon H. Harris, *Paul Cuffe, Black America and the African Return* (New York, 1972).

22.   The life of Thayendanegea is fully (but often inaccurately) told in William L. Stone, *The Life of Joseph Brant* (2 vols., Albany, N.Y., 1838); more modern treatments are Louis A. Wood, *The War Chief of the Six Nations; A Chronicle of Joseph Brant* (Toronto, 1920), and the sketch by Milledge L. Bonham in *The Dictionary of American Biography*, ed. Dumas Malone (22 vols., New York, 1928-58), II, 604-05.

23.   Barbara Graymont, *The Iroquois in the American Revolution* (Syracuse, N.Y., 1972), ch. 2-3; Georgina C. Nammack, *Fraud, Politics, and the Dispossession of the Indians; The Iroquois Land Frontier in the Colonial Period* (Norman, Okla., 1969).

24.   The much publicized visit of four Iroquois chiefs to London in 1710 is described in Richard P. Bond, *Queen Anne's American Kings* (Oxford, 1952).

25.   Graymont, *Iroquois in the American Revolution*, p. 109. Chapters 4 and 5 of this book provide an excellent account of how the powerful Iroquois, whose neutrality was the object of great exertions by the Continental Congress and its agents, threw in their lot with the British in 1776. Two Iroquois tribes, the Tuscaroras and Oneidas, sided with the Americans, thus splitting the Iroquois Confederacy, but the main Iroquois strength was ranged against the Americans throughout the war.

26.   Anthony F.C. Wallace, *The Death and Rebirth of the Seneca* (New York, 1972), p. 146. For a detailed account of the Iroquois war experience consult Graymont, *Iroquois in the American Revolution*, ch. 5-9.

27.   *Ibid.*, ch. 10; Wallace, *Death and Rebirth*, ch. 6-7.

28.   Although the basic problems of all Native Americans were much alike, tribal war experiences varied greatly, depending on proximity to British lines of supply, internal politics and leadership patterns, the ebb and flow of British-American fighting in particular areas, and other factors. The struggles of the northern tribes can be followed in Randolph C. Downes, *Council Fires on the Upper Ohio; A Narrative of Indian Affairs in the Upper Ohio Valley until 1795* (Pittsburgh, 1940); Francis Jennings, "The Indians' Revolution," in Young, ed., *The American Revolution*, pp. 319-48; C.A. Weslager, *The Delaware Indians: A History* (New Brunswick, N.J., 1972); and Graymont, *Iroquois in the American Revolution*. For the southern tribes the best of a large but conceptually weak literature includes James H. O'Donnell, III, *Southern Indians in the American Revolution* (Knoxville, Tenn., 1973); Thomas Perkins Abernathy, *Western Lands and the American Revolution* (New York, 1937); Corkran, *Creek Frontier;* Randolph C. Downes, "Cherokee-American Relations in the Upper Tennessee Valley, 1776-1791," *East Tennessee Historical Society Publications,* 8 (1936), 35-53; Arthur P. Whitaker, "Spain and the Cherokee Indians, 1783-1798," *North Carolina Historical Review,* 4 (1927), 252-67; A.V. Goodpasture, "Indian Wars and Warriors of the Old Southeast," *Tennessee Historical Magazine,* 4 (1918), 3-49, 106-45, 161-210, 252-89; Philip M. Hamer, "John Stuart's Indian Policy During the Early Months of the American Revolution," *Mississippi Valley Historical Review,* 17 (1930-31), 351-66; Edgar L. Pennington, "East Florida in the American Revolution, 1775-1783," *Florida Historical Quarterly,* 9 (1930), 24-46; and Arthur P. Whitaker, *The Spanish-American Frontier, 1783-1795; The Westward Movement and the Spanish Retreat in the Mississippi Valley* (Boston, 1927). The problem with most of these studies, especially those pertaining to the southern tribes, is that they are written as accounts of white-Indian relations during a

period of white revolutionary and post-revolutionary stress. Ethnohistorical analyses of most of the major tribes during the second half of the eighteenth century—a period of crucial importance in Indian history east of the Mississippi River—remain to be written.

29. For post-war American policies see Abernethy, *Western Lands*, ch. 22-26; Reginald Horsman, *The Frontier in the Formative Years, 1783-1815* (New York, 1970) and *Expansion and American Indian Policy, 1783-1812* (East Lansing, Mich., 1967); Walter H. Mohr, *Federal Indian Relations, 1774-1788* (Philadelphia, 1933); and Downes, *Council Fires*, ch. 12-13.

30. Quoted in Randolph C. Downes, "George Morgan, Indian Agent Extraordinary, 1776-1779," *Pennsylvania History*, I (1934), 202.

31. Writes one recent historian, whose work is helping to reconceptualize the field of Native American history: "...the American revolutionaries fought for empire over the west as well as for their own freedom in the east. While the colony-states fought for independence from the Crown, the tribes had to fight for independence from the states. It makes a huge embarrassment to ideology that the Revolution wore one face looking eastward across the Atlantic and another looking westward into the continent, but Indians have always obtruded awkardly from the smooth symmetry of historical rationalization." Jennings, "The Indians' Revolution," in Young, ed., *American Revolution*, p. 322.

32. McGillivray to James White, April 8, 1787, quoted in Caughey, *McGillivray*, p. 33.

33. Quoted in Reginald Horsman, "American Indian Policy in the Old Northwest, 1783-1812," *William and Mary Quarterly*, 3d ser., 18 (1961), 40.

34. Washington to James Duane, September 7, 1783, quoted in *ibid.*, p. 38.

3

Antecedents of the Mexican Independence Movement: Social Instability and Political Discord

Enrique Florescano

IT IS GENERALLY ACCEPTED, at least in the most basic analyses, that periods of economic crisis and impoverishment of the masses generate social malaise and political instability which encourage violent political movements. An extension of this thesis presupposes, on the other hand, that periods of economic growth lead to social harmony and political stability. This thesis would not serve, however, to explain the extraordinary and extremely unequal economic development of New Spain between 1750 and 1810, and would be even less useful in explaining the insurgent movement which erupted at the end of this period. The great administrative, political, economic and social transformations which the country witnessed during this period did not produce stability, nor was the movement of 1810 incited principally by a popular revolt intended to provide a solution to social and political afflictions.

The process of intensive economic growth and great social and political changes which occurred in New Spain between 1750 and 1810 seem more comprehensible following de Tocqueville's explanation of the French Revolution. The Revolution, he said in *The Ancien Regime and the French Revolution,* was preceded by "an advance in the prosperity of the nation as swift as it was undetected. This prosperity, in a steady and growing evolution, far from pacifying the population, promoted a spirit of unrest." The popular discontent was more intense in the areas of France which most benefitted from the gains. Later, Crane Brinton *(The Anatomy of Revolution,* 1938) and subsequent historians and political theorists have reinforced the thesis which points to accelerated economic growth as a factor which disrupts old structures and stimulates political expectations that lead to revolutionary transformations.

In our opinion, the political, administrative, and economic changes which New Spain experienced after 1750 provoked a social dislocation which, not finding institutional solutions through political avenues, and unable to reverse other processes which made the system's contradictions more evident, gave rise to the revolutionary movement which inflamed the country in 1810.

Here, briefly, are the primary factors introduced into the society of New Spain by rapid economic growth and the

Bourbon reforms which accompanied them, which created the social disequilibrium.

We begin with the maladjustments of an economic nature. In any society, even the most equitable in the distribution of the dividends of the social product, the process of accelerated economic development produces imbalances or alterations of a greater or lesser degree. In New Spain the era 1770-1800 produced a much more violent destabilizing effect, as much because it broke a very slow socio-economic readjustment which had begun more than a century before, as by issuing forth from an extremely unequal society. With these antecedents it could not be a stabilizing force but, on the contrary, an agitator and creator of more acute and obvious inequalities. One of its consequences was the displacement of economic growth and the concentration of wealth from the center of the country toward the Bajío and the west, provoking the start of economic marginalization of previously privileged regions, such as Puebla-Tlaxcala, and the ascendance of others, like Veracruz. This regional readjustment created new economic realities and political expectations not anticipated in the old system, which will be considered later. Another consequence, this one intended by the economic reforms of the Bourbons, was the strenghtening of the export sector of the colony (mining, commerce, agriculture for export) with the purpose of increasing dependence on the metropolis. The success of this policy, however, initiated various problems which the metropolis had not anticipated and which widened the gaps in the system. Thus, at the same time that economic reforms and fiscal policy made New Spain more of a colony than ever, the multiplier effect of these reforms on the internal economy of the country engendered in the people the certainty, on one hand, that the metropolis looked after its own interests, and that these were, in the majority of cases, contrary to the interests of the colony; and, on the other hand, that New Spain was self-sufficient, that its development and potentialities would be greater if she dispensed with her ties to Spain. This conviction was clearly expressed in one of the subversive *planes* issued prior to the explosion of 1810, signed by friar Melchor de Talamantes, in which he says that New Spain had "all the resources and facilities for the sustenance, maintenance, and happiness of its dwellers," and therefore must become independent, as the Spanish government was not concerned with the general welfare of New Spain. In other words, in the clash between the growth of external economic controls and the expansion and development of the internal sector of the economy, the privileges conceded to the former and the marginalization of the latter became more obvious among those who had not benefitted, and they were the majority.

We must emphasize that although the economic boom was fairly general, the distribution of its benefits was extremely unequal due to the tremendous existing social inequality. By sectors, the exclusive minority which controlled the activities most closely tied to the external sector (miners and merchants) received the highest income, while the majority of farmers, sweatshop workers, artisans, small businessmen, and laborers had to divide the earnings of a boom which to them was as spectacular as it was scarce in rewards. The ills and expectations instigated by this disproportionate distribution intensified, or acquired unforeseen aspects because of the policies which the Crown adopted in relation to certain groups. The power and privileged condition which the mine operators (mainly creoles) enjoyed were viewed negatively by the peninsular merchants (whose prerogatives were diminished) and by the creole agriculturalists and entrepreneurs who, in addition to having limited access to the larger earnings, had no access to the social and political rewards which were given to the Spaniards. Meanwhile, the tremendous blow dealt to the economic and political power of the merchants, in addition to earning for the metropolis the discontent of the strongest Spanish enclave in the colony, disrupted the entire system which gathered wealth and power into Mexico City, creating a vacuum which regional merchants and entrepreneurs, probably the natural enemies of the Capital merchants, hastened to fill. In short, on a regional level, as well as by sectors or groups, economic growth introduced grave disruptions in the system and promoted a more clearcut division between the diverse segments. This in turn produced a clearer awareness of their interests and antagonisms.

Accelerated economic growth acted as a disruptive agitator of groups and established economic classes, and as an active dissolvent of traditional social bonds. The intense and generalized pressure which in this period was exercised over the indigenous peoples had its equivalent only in the worst moments of the Conquest and the first years of colonization. Communal lands and property, family, ethnic and linguistic ties, and many of the chief social and cultural institutions which survived were displaced or broken by the accelerated process of economic change between 1750 and 1800. Communal lands suffered from the combined assault of expanding large estates and smaller ranches, from enormous pressures from new landless groups (castes and *mestizos*) and from the increased demands of the growing indigenous population itself. The loss or lack of land left a considerable part of the Indian population without roots, and it was quickly trapped by the enterprises of the capitalist centers which led the great transformation that spurred New Spain.

The large agricultural enterprises, sugar mills, and cattle ranches converted traditional peasants into peons and day laborers while the demand for unskilled workers in the mines and urban centers incorporated them into the semi-servile proletariat which formed rapidly in this period.

The process of disintegration of the Indian community was also seen in the extraordinarily high number of vagrant Indians which many towns recorded at the end of the century, and in the steady drift of men from the indigenous areas to the zones of greatest economic growth. Once-prosperous villages and previously stable communities, especially in the region of Puebla-Tlaxcala, were literally abandoned. From this period also dates the formation on a large scale of a mobile rural proletariat which traveled a yearly circuit from cotton to sugar to tobacco plantation or performed seasonal work on the agricultural estates or cattle ranches.

Another source of social discord induced by the rapid economic growth was the appearance of new groups not included in the established order. The castes, groups of varying racial mixture, which toward the end of the eighteenth century comprised twenty-two percent of the total population (slightly more than 1,300,000 individuals of all colors) exemplify this phenomenon. It was probably, along with the creoles, the most rapidly growing ethnic group and that which encountered, on the part of Spaniards, creoles, and Indians, the most hostility to its social integration. A discordant group, lacking a distinctive economic, social, or cultural base, its attempts to carve a niche in any of the small worlds within its reach failed. This in turn created more instability and resentment, which converted the racially-mixed segments into the problem groups of the last period of the viceroyalty. Much less numerous, but of greater political danger, were the "new rich" who were born with the boom. These individuals, provincial merchants, agriculturists, entrepreneurs, or miners, adapted poorly to the system, which often rejected them, and always threatened the system by demanding political and social status in keeping with their new economic position.

It is not likely, however, that these extensive dislocations in the economic situation of the regions, classes, and sectors could have given rise to political instability if the colonial system had provided adequate channels of social mobility and flexible political institutions, which would have diminished or absorbed the tensions instigated by the rapid and unequal growth. But one of the most obvious characteristics of the system was its rigid social stratification. The system only accepted the movement of individuals from lower groups to higher strata through a scrupulous screening made on an individual basis which presumed total acceptance of the values of the higher strata. The social bonds created by dominant group acceptance and skin color, rather than becoming less important, became more inflexible as a response to the social pretentions of the new groups which threatened the monopoly of the oligarchy. On finding the possibilities of ascent and social mobility so hermetically sealed, a considerable portion of creoles, mestizos, and castes (to whom the economic boom had brought benefits and created new expectations) found themselves with growing social frustrations.

The social frustrations faced by this group were matched by a parallel process of political frustration. In this process, as well as in the inelasticity of the political system itself, the policies adopted by the Bourbons had a hand. The Bourbon reforms increased the social and political frustrations in various ways. On the one hand, they denied creoles and mestizos the posts and political jobs that their own representatives had been given, removed them from positions previously enjoyed in the Royal Audencia (judiciary), in the public treasury, and in the administration of government agencies on various levels, impeded their access to high military and ecclesiastic offices, ultimately alienating them in an increasingly systematic way from any position of power. On the other hand, the Crown placed Spaniards in the highest posts and in those newly created by the reforms. The inflexible application of both policies, just when the expectations of participation on the part of creoles and mestizos were highest, plunged them into the worst frustration, making them see, at the same time, that only a change spawned in and directed by the colony would be able to transform the existing state of things.

However, the closing of opportunities for creoles and mestizos was complete only at the highest levels. The intermediate and lower offices in administration, church, and army were multiplied by economic growth and by the Bourbon reforms, and there frustration became most evident, and concrete forms of political activity began to be defined. Outcasts from political life, but having access to the municipal councils, the lower-level priests and lower- and middle-level military began to change these institutions into political bodies for the defense of their interests. The most outstanding case was that of the municipal council, an institution lacking any real personality or political independence for more than two and one-half centuries, which the creoles revived as a democratic body and proposed later as the political instrument endowed with sovereignty and representative faculties. This transformation of the council is expressed with great clarity in the "Representation Made by the City of Mexico to King,

Charles III, in 1771, concerning preference for creoles over Europeans in the distribution of jobs and benefits in these kingdoms." This transformation acquires political importance in the events of 1808, when, facing the abdication of the Spanish monarch, the council of Mexico City, assuming a role as representative of the whole kingdom, proposed that the Viceroy continue provisionally in the government until a meeting of all the municipal councils of the viceroyalty should decide on another solution. From this position on the part of the council arose the crisis that terminated with the deposing of Viceroy Iturrigaray.

The participation of priests and creole army officials in the conspiracies prior to 1810 is as well known. Nevertheless, the step which bridged social frustration and active political participation of this group is not explainable without the intervention of a third factor which precipitated the formation of political consciousness. This factor was modernity, the penetration into New Spain of the ideas and culture of the *Siglo de las Luces*. Alongside all the other processes noted in this essay, between 1750 and 1800 the philosophy of the Enlightenment which proposed a new conception of society, of the State, and of the individual, was introduced into the Viceroyalty. The Holy Office of the Inquisition was the first to denounce the presence of this dangerous, destabilizing agent: the growing infiltration of the works of Rousseau, Voltaire, Diderot, and others who disseminated new political ideas or attacked the traditional scholastic-Aristotelian philosophy. And even though the Inquisition took measures against the invasion of the "heretical and seditious ideas," its attempt was frustrated by the spirit of the age which had penetrated all sectors of society and, above all, the members of the Church itself. The principal instructors of the new ideas and customs were, first of all, the governors and functionaries charged with implementing the Bourbon reforms. Beginning with the Marquis de Croix, who assumed office in 1766, almost all of the viceroys, in greater or lesser measure, were enthusiastic followers of the Enlightenment: Bucareli, Mayorgo, the two Gálvez, Nuñez de Haro y Peralta, Flores, Revilla Gigedo, Azanza. These men, chosen by the ministers of Charles III to carry out the reform policies of Enlightened Despotism in New Spain, took with them the political, social, religious, and economic ideas of the *Siglo de las Luces* and disseminated them in their courts, at frequent literary gatherings, at their soirées which provoked many scandals, and through the retinue of Francophile followers that accompanied them: barbers, tailors, cooks, valets, and others. In the studies of the period and of the government of these viceroys the opposition which they encountered in implementing the policies they came to institute has been emphasized, but similar studies analyzing the tremendous "demonstration effect" which these ideas and acts had on the lower social classes which observed them are lacking, an effect which can be evaluated in the denunciations of the corruption of manners due to the spread of French habits and styles. On this level, the adoption of the French mode of dress, the increase in social gatherings, coffee houses and billiard rooms, and the spread of parties and balls, had a destructive effect on the traditional norms and precepts which was much more corrosive than the diffusion of more revolutionary works. It is superfluous to mention that those who adopted these habits with the greatest passion and speed were the new rich and the emergent urban middle class, that is to say, the groups which the growth of the last years had helped to form.

Of similar importance, although less well-known,

were the actions of many high officials, men such as Ramón Posada (financial officer of the Royal Treasury), José Mangino (superintendent of the Mint), Fausto de Elhuyar (director of the School of Mining) and those acting as intendents and provincial governors. Some, active popularizers of the new ideas, made a concerted effort to put them into practice, which provoked serious public conflicts and personal crises. To incorporate in one's daily life the principles of enlightened despotism, to apply social philanthropy, to reconstruct on rational lines the administration and the public treasury, or merely to fight the monopolies, meant for these men to engage in struggles with the interests and the established groups most directly tied to the peninsula. Further, when their own activity, or that of the creoles who shared their ideas, demanded that they go beyond a simple formal declaration of principles and ideas, these high officials often encountered serious personal conflicts. To carry the adopted principles to their logical consequence implied support of a policy which went against the interests of the Crown. Perhaps the intendents and provincial officials suffered most intensely from these internal conflicts and clashes. The narrow confines of their provincial surroundings and the immediate hostility created between them and the traditional groups led them to join the natural challengers to the system: the creoles, Juan Antonio de Riaño, the Intendent of Guanajuato, gathered in his house for dinners or literary discussions many of the Querétaro conspirators, and was a personal friend of Miguel Hidalgo, whose ill-clad followers were to slay the illustrious intendent in later years.

The members of the most powerful and traditional institution in the colony were not immune to the winds of modernity. The initial battle, made more difficult for being isolated and misunderstood, was unleashed by the Jesuits, who pursued it beyond the time of their expulsion in 1767. José Rafael Campoy (1723-1777), Francisco Javier Alegre (1729-1788), Diego José Abad (1727-1779) and Francisco Javier Clavijero (1731-1787), were the prime movers behind the great attack on the traditional scholastic philosophy, until then the official philosophy and the only one taught. Their teachings and writings introduced the following changes: the first systematic criticism of scholastic methods and dogmas, acceptance of new European philosophical currents, the introduction of modern, experimental physics in courses on philosophy, development of scientific eclecticism, the adoption of new methodological orientations in philosophical reflection as well as in teaching.

With the Jesuits expelled, the process of philosophic and mental renewal in the ranks of the Church was continued by Father Juan Benito Gamarra, who quickly converted the Colégio de San Francisco de Sales de San Miguel el Grande into a center of modernism, incorporating into the curriculum the materials which were transforming knowledge in Europe. Because of his reform activities, as well as his authorship of revisionist works of high prestige in this period (*Elementa Recentionis Philosophie*, 1774; *Academias filosóficas*, 1774; and *Errores del entendimiento humano*, 1781), Gamarra focused on himself, as had the Jesuits before him, the assaults of traditional minds. Denounced the Holy Office for free-thinking, he escaped unharmed from the crisis through the strong support of higher officials of the Church, among them the Bishop of Michoacán, Luis Fernández de Hoyos, and even from the Inquisition, which silenced his accusers. His triumph marks the moment in which the renovating ideas were imposed on the traditional in the heart of the most conservative institution. From then on, despite the continuation of denunciations, attacks, and persecutions on the part of the most recalcitrant members of the clergy, the propagation of modern philosophy and science could not be stopped. In the schools and seminaries of Michoacán and Guadalajara, reformist centers such as that in San Miguel el Grande took hold. Even in the University of Mexico and in the academies of the capital, the most traditional institutions, hesitant innovations in educational methods appeared, and the door to revisionist authors and their works was opened. Another obvious sign of change was the failure of the Holy Office to repress and contain the circulation of prohibited works. The second half of the eighteenth century witnessed the circulation of these works and the spread of their readers beyond ecclesiastics—from the highest levels to the most humble friars, including members of the Inquisition—to members of the military, the aristocracy, functionaries and professionals of the middle class. Another significant fact is that while in the first half of the century religious studies were considered damaging or heretical, in the second half the majority of these writings were of philosophical-political bent, and by the end of the century predominantly of a political nature.

In this transformation of the colonial mentality, a conspicuous role was played by the arrival of Spanish prelates who openly sympathized with the ideas of the Enlightenment. Archbishops such as Antonio de Lorenzana (1722-1804) and Alonso de Haro y Peralta (1729-1800), and Bishops like Francisco Fabián y Fuero (1719-1801) and Luis Fernández de Hoyos (?-1775) of Puebla and Michoacán respectively, in addition to supporting reform tendencies within the Church, attempted to give them a more social and philanthropic bent. The vanguard of the Church in religious and humanistic matters was the bishopric of Michoacán, the same region where, a little more than two and one-half centuries earlier, Vasco de Quiroga had attempted to establish a community based on the principles of Thomas More's *Utopia*. Between 1770 and 1810 the episcopal seat of this diocese was occupied by a series of notable prelates who united modern enlightened and philanthropic ideas with the desire to put them into practice. Bishops Luis Fernández de Hoyos, Antonio de San Miguel (1726-1804), and Manuel Abad y Queipo (1751-1825), together with José Pérez Calama (1740-1792), promoted an extensive transformation in the way of thinking of the diocese, which ecompassed the introduction of modern philosophy and the consequent rejection of the scholastic, the creation of academies and seminaries devoted to new programs of study, the development of a "politico-charitable philosophy" to be applied to land matters, the importation and diffusion of Spanish liberalism in social and economic matters, and the formation of a large group of priests and teachers imbued with these ideas. Without the union of these reform elements, it would be difficult to explain the progressive socio-economic writings of the Bishops San Miguel and Abad y Queipo, in which there appears a precise presentation of the causes which keep the Indians and castes in their degrading situation, as well as the first lucid analysis of the problem of the large landed estates and of their harmful impact on the social body. Nearly all of the economic and social problems which confronted the development of the colony were reviewed with clarity and penetration in the writings of the bishops. The necessity to abolish the infamous condition of the castes and to give them free status was argued in the writings of Abad y Queipo, along with the suitability of ending the paternalistic legislation which protected the Indians, of dividing the communal lands and of permitting direct contact and mixture of the Indians with other ethnic groups in order to ensure their incorporation in the "progress." At the same time, in the writings of Pérez Calama and in his tireless daily work, could be seen the obsessive effort of this generation to break out of the traditional mentality, to introduce immediately the ideals of the Enlightenment, and to create the conditions in which these ideas might be applied to the surrounding reality. Thus Pérez Calama stood out first as a reformer of curricula in Puebla (where he was rector of the Colégio Palafoxiano under the protection of the Bishop, Fabián y Fuero) and Michoacán; later as a popularizer of modern philosophy and of the Enlightenment through his sermons, instructional letters, and short works on Christian policy designed to conquer the "ignorance and coarseness" of the parish priests of Michoacán; and finally as an active follower of his own ideas in promoting the foundation of a Society of the Friends of the Country in Valladolid (the first in New Spain), and in trying to create industries and useful activies which would provide work for the needy classes and elevate the economic condition of the region. He was, moreover, responsible for the plan of "extraordinary plantings" and other philanthropic measures which alleviated the terrible suffering in Michoacán when the area was scourged by the great famine of 1785-1786.

But, as frequently happens with generations confronted with the double task of undermining the foundations of a tradition and of lighting the pathways to the future, the generation of governors, public officials, and Spanish clerics which led New Spain between 1770 and 1810 suffered the bitter frustrations of contradiction and internal discord. The majority of them had to make an about face when the independence of the English colonies to the north and the triumph and radicalization of the French Revolution taught the people of New Spain that the implementation of the principles of the Enlightenment meant forging new political and social realities. Of those who had advanced the reform of the mind and circulated the new ideas which were changing the era, the priests and prelates suffered more than anyone else during the painful transition which the country would undergo. The figure of Abad y Queipo encapsulates the contradictions and clashes of his generation. Student and direct heir of the enlightened and renewing sermons of Bishop San Miguel and of the Cantor Pérez Calama, a perceptive observer of the social and economic distortions of the colonial system, and its most lucid critic and foe, he will be, at a later date, the excommunicator of Hidalgo, the assassin of the most perfect and coherent product his generation had given birth to.

Nevertheless, this generation of enlightened governors carried out well its job as bridge between a world which was splitting apart at the seams and another whose outlines they helped to reveal. Between 1790 and 1810 the diffusion of ideas and the social ferment were more intense than ever in New Spain. Criticism of scholasticism and of old traditions gave way to criticism of social, political, and economic conditions in the colony. The centers of discontent and agitation were the academies and seminaries, the curates and the new media of diffusion. The agents of subversion were the priests, lawyers, and creole military; the regions where the discontents accumulated and the conspiracies multiplied were the most prosperous and the most disrupted by the sudden economic growth (the Bajío and Michoacán, Guadalajara).

The explosion which hurled the country into the

modern era has as its antecedent these three processes which we have tried to outline in the preceding pages: a rapid economic growth which disrupted social structures forged over a century of slow adjustment and which made existing inequalities more obvious; an almost total inflexibility in the political and social fabric which neither gave room to new groups nor absorbed the contradictions and expectations created by the aforementioned process; and an accelerated dissemination of the ideas of modernism which encouraged alienated groups to design and rationalize their vindication. It is no accident that the area of the Bajío and Michoacán, which experienced the greatest economic growth, contained the highest concentration of creoles and harbored the most advanced centers of intellectual renovation, was the matrix of the insurrection headed by Hidalgo.

4

The
Continental Congress
and the
Nationalization
of American Politics

H. James Henderson

THE AMERICAN REVOLUTION, because it was at least partly a colonial war for independence, shared with Mexico and other emergent colonial nations the problem of reconciling territorial boundaries with a manageable political system. And in common with other nations emerging from colonial status, the United States had to determine what sort of nation it would become. The answer to the second question was deceptively simple for the revolting North American colonies—a republic, of course. All the thirteen colonies that became part of the United States had experience with representative government in their colonial assemblies; and of all the two dozen British-American colonies only those with such experience and with territorial contiguity became part of the American Revolution.

Territorially contiguous republican governments, then, described the shape and internal structure of the new nation, an answer that seemed to emerge naturally during the resistance to British innovations in imperial policy during the 1760s and 1770s. But British-Americans during that resistance had repudiated Parliament because it was too distant and too unrepresentative, so that the logic of their argument that did so much to define the extent and structure of the new nation mitigated against consolidation of power at the national level. In a word, the requirements for nationhood called for the creation of the weakest sort of national authority.

Nor were there other political forces that could fill the vacuum. The colonies had no vital center—no Paris, and no London that provided a geographic and administrative focus for the new nation. Philadelphia was the most likely candidate for that role. It was the largest colonial city and its location was reasonably close to the center of the widely flung settlements along the Atlantic coast. But its population was small by comparison with the major European capitals and its economic influence did not radiate much beyond southern New Jersey, Pennsylvania, Delaware and northern Maryland. Further, to the extent that it did become a major center for the management of the Revolution, it was rendered suspect in the more extended parts of the Confederation. Nor did the new nation have a single figure who could provide cohesion and leadership. Despite the enormous popularity, even adulation, that surrounded Washington as the years went by, his importance as a revolutionary leader is minor by comparison with Simón

Bolívar, for example. Nor did the United States have a "Party of the Revolution" with the organization and discipline that supplies cohesion to a revolutionary movement. There was a Patriot "party" of sorts, and its influence was often decisive, but it was a rather loose association of differently constituted radical elements in the thirteen colonies that took the form of a popular force, or movement, rather than an organized party. Political interests that coalesced during the Revolution claimed to represent the Patriot tradition, but the fact that this sort of authenticity was claimed by such disparate aggregations as New England parochialists and middle states centralists is ample evidence of the diffuseness of this "party."

American Revolutionaries did have a critically important body of ideology that provided an indispensible vocabulary that animated as well as legitimized the movement toward independence. But while this ideology helped greatly in bringing distrust and resentment against the mother country to a pitch, and while it helped substantially to awaken Americans to the qualitative separation between their societies and that of Britain, a separation that had evolved during the previous century, it could not prescribe uniform and specific solutions for the creation of a national republic. Republican ideology, as Robert Shallope has contended, was a "vague and supple" persuasion embracing terms such as "virtue" and "character" that were susceptible to many different interpretations.

The problem for the Continental Congress, was to make thirteen revolutions into one—thirteen republics into one. Because of the weakness of Congress it was an impossible task, of course, and the politics of the Confederation were nationalized only to the extent that there were common concerns that were beyond the capacity of the individual states to handle. The war, diplomacy, the management of the West, and, with qualifications, the management of the common debt, were such concerns, and these were the materials from which the politics of the Revolution were nationalized. These were parameters that were severely constricted by comparison with the sphere of action accorded to the national government under the Constitution, but they amounted to a greater press of external authority than Americans had been accustomed to, and clearly they were sufficient to activate partisan politics.

Predictably, those politics would involve sectional strains, for a basic difficulty in effecting a colonial war for independence was putting together a unified effort from disparate parts. But, as we are now beginning to understand from the research of historians who are investigating the local history and demographic trends of colonial America, there were other strains that plausibly would become enmeshed in the nationalization of American politics. Kenneth Lockridge has hypothesized that the modernization of American society that was occurring as a consequence of overcrowding, diversification, economic polarization and so forth, could have contributed to the partial and begrudging acceptance of an ideology of acquisitive individualism in place of the traditional republican emphasis upon a virtuous citizenry, and that inadvertantly the Constitution embodied this ideological transformation. The question naturally arises: was the Continental Congress sufficiently responsive to these or other changes and strains in the society to embody national politics to a degree hardly predicated by the structure of the Articles of Confederation?

The answer to that question, in the light of the history of Congressional debates, resolutions and acts, would seem to be a qualified "yes." Hardly an issue arose in the

Federal Congress of the 1790s that was not prefigured by actions of the Continental Congress. Hamilton's fiscal program was anticipated almost entirely by the proposals and accomplishments of Robert Morris during his tenure as Superintendent of Finance. The location of the national capital, the question of discriminatory tariffs against the foreign nations with which the United States had no treaty, the status of the navigation of the Mississippi, and even the matter of taxes on land and slaves as well as excises and duties for revenue were all considered or enacted by the Continental Congress.

Despite the fact that for pragmatic reasons the rule was established in the first Continental Congress that voting would be by states rather than population, the Congress was more representative than this agreement (incorporated of course in the Articles of Confederation) would imply. Large states, simply because they had a greater tax base than the small states, almost invariably maintained larger delegations in the Congress than did the smaller states. Since the Congress did most of its work through committees, it was inevitable that states such as Massachusetts, New York, Pennsylvania, and Virginia should dominate congressional business. And they did. In making appointments to important posts overseas, a matter Congress considered especially crucial, only in the appointments of Silas Deane of Connecticut and Henry Laurens of South Carolina was the second tier of states represented. The major administrative posts in finance, foreign affairs and war were dominated by representatives of the major states. The sovereign and independent states of Georgia and Delaware may have been the equals of Massachusetts and Virginia under the Articles, but they had only a fraction of the influence of their larger partners in the affairs of Congress.

Rhode Island was a notable exception to this rule. Despite her small size, she was represented by delegates who were unusually vocal and frequently troublesome from the perspective of some of the delegates from the larger states. This fact illuminates another dimension of congressional politics that makes those politics more sensitive to the mobilized activated population than the structure of the Articles would suggest. Rhode Island was a highly commercialized state with substantial stakes in the decisions of the national government; and because of this, her influence was larger than her size. Representation, though theoretically equal, was responsive both to population and other factors such as commercial interest. Some Congressional delegations, most notably those from Pennsylvania and New York, reflected whatever party or interest happened to be in command of the state assembly at the time delegates were elected. The result could be an abrupt change in the ideological posture of the state in Congress, as when the localist delegations of the late seventies from Pennsylvania were replaced by the nationalist "Republicans" during the early eighties.

In short, although the Congress was meant to represent states, and not the people, and though its charter as a diplomatic assembly *did* affect its actions, it was sufficiently responsive to the hypothetical national constituency to illuminate some of the internal strains that accompanied the Revolution as well as contests between the states.

This representativeness of the Congress was largely inadvertant and far from complete. It was rare that opposite "parties" were represented in a single delegation at the same time, and in some delegations such as those from South Carolina important and substantial interests were systematically excluded. (Of the thirty delegates elected to Congress from South Carolina between 1774 and 1789, twenty-six were from Charleston.) All that I am suggesting is that we may be able to better understand the social and ideological contours of the Revolution by looking at the political process in the Continental Congress while disregarding its formal structure as an assembly of sovereign states.

II

The basic configuration of partisan politics in the Continental Congress was regional; most fundamentally, the struggle was between the North and the South. Some of the sources of these divisions can be found in obvious state and sectional interests. New England, Massachusetts in particular, was much more concerned about gaining access to the fisheries off Nova Scotia and Newfoundland in the peace negotiations than was the South, and when the French Minister, Conrad Alexandre Gérard, pressured Congress to eliminate rights to the fisheries from the peace terms, it was the South (and the middle states too) that supported, and New England that adamantly opposed, following Gérard's advice. The middle states and New England held substantially more of the Confederation debt than did the South, and, unsurprisingly, delegates from the North had a keener interest in supporting that debt with national revenue than did delegates from the South. The South, on the other hand, had a greater stake in securing the navigation of the Mississippi than did the North because of its extensive western claims.

Thus the early nationalization of American politics in the Congress involved the clarification and compromise, when possible, of regional interests. This was a normal occurrence in the politics of a new nation, and it did not terminate with the Confederation. The assumption of state debts and the struggle over the location of the national capital involved North-South trade-offs in the First Federal Congress. More, the first party system as it emerged during the early nineties had distinct regional contours.

There were other dimensions of Congressional politics. During the period between 1775 and 1779 Congress was disproportionately influenced by a coalition dominated by New Englanders with allies from the more radical elements of the middle states and scattered support from the South, most notably the Lees of Virginia. This period of New England (or "Eastern" as the New England states were often called then) ascendency began with an exuberant expectation that the energies of regenerative republicanism would not only perfect society and politics but also expel the enemy. Because the latter had actually happened in Boston in the spring of 1976, and because it was a predominantly Eastern army that materialized to defeat Burgoyne at Saratoga in 1777, the Easterners, who had been the foremost advocates of the ideology of regenerative republicanism with its Puritanical emphasis on austerity and virtue, seemed to have been supported by the events.

But by 1779 Congressional finances were well on the way toward collapse in the midst of hyper-inflation of Continental monies that had been issued without certain promise of redemption. The Congress could not tax and the states failed to deliver their assigned quotas. At about this time the prospects of victory were enhanced by the entry of France into the war, but the diplomatic terms set forth by France created profound divisions in Congress. Altogether, it was a situation that called for pragmatic rather than purist solutions, and in a reorientation of policy made easier by the departure of many of the Eastern ideologues, Congress tightened its administration by creating executive boards. The most influential and significant executive office was that of Superintendent of Finance under the direction of Robert Morris. Morris extracted substantial discretionary powers from Congress as a result of support not only from the middle states delegations, which now had seized the mantle of leadership from New England, but also from the South.

After a series of ingenious and partially successful attempts to nationalize Congressional finance and administration, Morris and the middle states party had to give up. Their central objective of securing an independent revenue for Congress through 5 percent duty on imported goods failed to be ratified by all the states. As the army demobilized without its back pay and assurances of officers' pensions some nationalists in Congress may have hoped that the resentments of the soldiers might be channeled toward an alteration of the Articles, but Washington firmly suppressed any potential coup d'etat at Newburgh, and the nationalists retired from Congress.

The years after the peace treaty were difficult for the new nation. Nonetheless, in the interval that followed the failure of the centralists from the middle states, a number of able Southerners arrived in Congress, most notably Jefferson, Monroe, and Charles Pinckney. Their appearance was hardly coincidental, for the South had a great stake in the management of the West that had been secured in the peace treaty. Southern leadership, particularly that of Jefferson, was instrumental in framing the great land ordinances, although not without important New England involvement. Southerners, notably James Monroe and Charles Pinckney, were also conspicuous for proposing commercial powers for the Continental Congress that would have greatly strengthened the national government. The commercial conferences at Mount Vernon and Annapolis set the stage for the Constitutional Convention in which debate was structured by the plan proposed by the Virginian delegation.

Thus, in very broad terms, the history of Congress seemed to go through three phases associated with the major sections of the new nation. Each offered what could be understood as a mode of nationalizing American politics: New England's stress on republican regeneration, localist and suspicious of consolidated power; the pragmatic bureaucratic centralism of the middle states nationalists; and the policy of westward expansion and commercial regulation proposed by the Southerners.

It is possible that this sequence was the result of the location of hostilities at specific moments in time. The war began in New England when the ideological fervor of republican reformation was at a peak. That the British were repulsed in early 1776 seemed to confirm the work of republican reformation. Later, when that fervor subsided, and when it became necessary to draw upon additional resources the war was located further south. It happened that in 1780 and 1781, after five years and more of warfare, the British struck at Virginia for the first time with concentrated strength. Their raids and campaigns were devastatingly successful until Cornwallis was trapped with the aid of the French fleet and army and Washington's Continentals who marched down from New York. The Virginia Assembly seriously considered creating a dictator to marshall the resources of the state, so far had the Revolution progressed. Thomas Jefferson, whose recollection of the event had to be particularly painful since he had been the Governor of Virginia at the initiation of those hostilities, reprobated the assembly for having contemplated "treason against the people... treason against mankind in general ... by giving their oppressors a proof, which they would have trumpeted through the universe, of the imbecility of republican government, in times of pressing danger, to shield them from harm."

But that the Virginians were willing to contemplate a dictator at home, and that they advocated nationalist proposals in Congress, was not simply an accidental result of their encountering the foe after the heady days of regenerative, purist republicanism had passed. Virginia's weakness had more to do with the relationship between citizens and their government than the tempo of war and republican ideology—a relationship that involved the contours of local political cultures which in turn, I am going to suggest, affected the process whereby American politics were nationalized in the Confederation and Federal periods.

III

So as to reduce regional comparisons to a manageable level, I have chosen two local constituencies in Virginia and Massachusetts that were later designated as congressional districts. The two localities had comparable populations that were large enough to be representative of the older, established local political cultures of those two states. A comparison of those two cultures may help to illuminate what the difficulties were in the problem of nation-building.

The Virginia constituency is the sixteenth congressional district including Caroline, Essex, Middlesex, King and Queen, and King William Counties in the middle region of the tidewater between the York and Rappahanock Rivers. The Massachusetts constituency is the third middle district in northeastern Massachusetts including eighteen towns in Essex and Middlesex Counties.

Each of these constituencies was located in the eastern region of its respective state; both were settled early (roughly from the 1630s to 1660s); both had access to the sea and were consequently commercialized economies; and each was indirectly represented in the Continental Congress: Edmund Pendleton, Meriwether Smith and Arthur Lee served from Virginia; and Elbridge Gerry, Samuel Holten, Stephen Higginson and Nathan Dane from Massachusetts. Both areas were strongly Patriot during the movement toward the Revolution. Both had relatively homogenous free populations; neither was marked by severe internal strain; and both were suffering economically relative to the more prosperous colonies. Thus in the resistance movement these Virginian and Massachusetts localities had a great deal in common—a fact that is instructive regarding the roles played by Virginia and Massachusetts in the coming of the Revolution.

Demographically, however, the two polities varied greatly. The Virginia district had a larger population (a function of the three-fifths clause)—some 48,000 as contrasted with 33,000 in the third middle district of Massachusetts. But the population density in Virginia was much lower—about thirty persons per square mile to some ninety persons in Massachusetts. Both were primarily agricultural, but the Massachusetts region was much more commercially developed and economically diversified, especially in the coastal towns of Salem and Marblehead. There were urban places in the Virginia district too, including Port Royal (Pendleton's residence) in Caroline County, Tappahanock in Essex County, and Urbanna (Lee's home) in Middlesex. All three towns were located on the broad Rappahanock River that was navigable by oceangoing vessels. But these Virginian towns were not much more than hamlets of a few hundred persons performing minimal urban functions as tobacco distribution centers and county seats. The towns do not change the most striking characteristic of the Virginia district, its dispersion.

The scattered character of the population helps to explain why Virginia was so vulnerable to military penetration. This region between the York and Rappahanock Rivers contained some 1500 square miles, but it had just 4800 white adult males (16 and over), about half of whom were enrolled in the militia. The Massachusetts district was much smaller, about 320 square miles, but it had a free adult male population of 8200. The character of the population in the two areas also differed. White adult males in the Massachusetts district accounted for over 24 percent of the total population, while in the Virginia district because of the presence of large numbers of slaves, free adult white males amounted to only about 10 percent of the total.

These two local political cultures were sharply different in the density and quality of community life. A Virginian might belong to many communities—the parish, the county, the plantation if it happened to be a large one, the town or hamlet if he happened to be part of that small minority who lived in one, or even the whole province if he belonged to the elite that resided part of the year in the capital while conducting business or serving in the assembly. But if for no other reason than the substantial distances that parishes and counties encompassed, community involvement for most was relatively low, as communities realized themselves only infrequently and partially. Religious life was lax, except for increasing numbers of dissenting congregations which, as Rhys Isaacs has perceptively shown, could take the form of rather intense communities within the diffuse Virginian community life. The county court met for part of one week a month, but those who had no business in court did not lightly make a round trip that averaged twenty to twenty-five miles. For some the journey was over sixty miles. In Massachusetts there was no confusion over the locus of the community. It was in the town that religious and political life materialized, where schools were organized, and where taxes were raised. Towns varied in size but on the average they were small enough for most healthy people to walk to town meetings. Whether or not towns were "peaceable kingdoms" as described by Michael Zuckerman, or were experiencing strain as a result of modernization (and both kinds of towns existed in northeastern Massachusetts during the era of the Revolution), the level of community interaction was vastly greater than in Virginia.

Virginia's low level of community life was joined to a system of politics in which a larger amount of discretion was lodged in the hands of local political elites than was true in Massachusetts towns. Although it is easy to exaggerate the democratic character of New England town life, town officials were elected (frequently by secret ballot), and taxes were approved (and frequently rejected or altered), by the town meeting. In Virginia, on the other hand, the county magistrates who levied and managed the taxes were appointed, and the vestries of the parishes who managed poor relief before the disestablishment of the Episcopal Church were self-perpetuating bodies. It was a system that created an elite with considerably more self-assurance than many less secure New England leaders could muster.

The Virginia elite along the Rappahanock also had a higher socio-economic status than did their Massachusetts counterparts in the towns of Essex and Middlesex Counties.

While the disparities in wealth were just as great in Salem as they were in the Virginia counties (indeed greater, for Salem had a growing number of impoverished inhabitants at the same time that the taxable wealth of rich merchants such as Richard Derby was increasing), in the more agricultural towns such as Reading and Woburn the largest farmers seldom held more than 200 acres. By contrast, all of Virginia counties along the Rappahanock had large landowners with prestigous family names such as Carter, Wormeley, Beverley, and Lee. Muscoe Garnett held some 4000 acres in Essex County—fully 2½ percent of the land in the county. Slaveholding was fairly widespread among the free tithables. In King William County 385 of 581 free tithables held at least 1 slave 16 years old or over, but of that 65 percent who owned slaves just 10 percent owned over half of the total. The really wealthy planters such as Garnett held from 100 to 200 slaves, and since slaves were the major source of wealth in a planter's estate, their elevation over the poor whites was much greater than the distance between the most prosperous and the poorest of a town like Woburn.

But in many ways the most striking and politically interesting difference between the two local political cultures had to do with taxes, or put differently, the socialized segment of the community's wealth. It should be stressed that during normal times direct taxes paid by the ordinary inhabitant of both Virginia and Massachusetts went largely to the local government. It was the town, the parish, and the county that provided the major services, including public works, welfare, police (a minor function in the eighteenth century), courts, support for religion (in both Virginia and Massachusetts until the church was disestablished in Virginia during the Revolution), and education (in Massachusetts only).

The support of local government in the Rappahanock counties was so much lower than in the towns of the third middle district of Massachusetts that the two local political cultures seem hardly comparable. Middlesex County, Virginia, with 1531 tithables (indicating a total population of about 3890) raised £477 in taxes in 1772 for the support of all parish and county services, including maintenance of the church. The town of Salem in Massachusetts with a population of about 5330 voted £1500 for the poor and schools and "necessary charges" alone (excluding church support). Nor was this peculiar to the most cosmopolitan towns. The smaller and more provincial town of Acton further inland taxed its inhabitants at a level of 4 shillings per capita before the Revolution and as high as $1.33 per capita by 1798. Per capita support in Middlesex was about half the first figure and one-quarter of the second. After the Revolution local taxes subsided sharply in the Rappahanock counties, largely due to the disestablishment of the vestries, but not entirely for that reason. Taxes for the support of the poor in Middlesex were lower per poll during the years 1800-1804 than they had been in either the 1690s or the 1750s. What happened in Middlesex probably confirmed the warning of Muscoe Garnett, Paul Nicholl and others from Middlesex who petitioned the assembly in support of an establishment for the vestries lest the poor be "left alone to Solicit the Cold hand of Charity." Our information about poor relief in Virginia during this period is extremely sketchy because records of the overseers of the poor, the elected officials who replaced the church wardens as supervisors of welfare, are difficult to find and often nonexistent. It is apparent, however, that not all countries gave such limited support to the poor. Albemarle County, whose population was increasing more rapidly than that of Middlesex, raised its tax for poor relief from 6 pounds of tobacco per poll to 12½ pounds between 1774 and 1803. Still, the higher figure represents only 15 cents per capita while in Charlestown, Massachusetts, citizens paid 41 cents per capita after the war. Actually, all kinds of local taxes, far from going down, steadily rose in Massachusetts towns as prosperity returned during the 1790s. In Salem local taxes went up from £3000 to £4500 between 1790 and 1799, a rise of 50 percent, while the population increased only 19 percent. In Reading and Acton there were comparable increases.

There are a number of interrelated reasons for these sharp differences between two long established local cultures in Virginia and Massachusetts. Slavery had a profound effect upon the costs of local government. Slaves (through their masters, of course) contributed taxes without receiving any of the social benefits from them, and this cut expenses in half. Space was another factor, although its influence was curiously opposite from what one might expect. With the great distances that separated people one from another and from their seat of government, it might be anticipated that highway and bridge costs would be higher than in a compactly settled Massachusetts town, but town costs were many times higher. The town of Reading with 18 square miles spent an average of £300 on roads in the 1790s while Essex County, thirteen times its size, spent less. Virginians seemed almost to relish their isolation. Another reason is that Virginia was capital-poor as are most dispersed agricultural societies. Indeed, the Salem merchant Elias Haskett Derby's stock in trade was worth more than all of Essex County's 153,000 acres (calculated at 10 shillings an acre).

From another angle of vision, one which subsumes these matters of slavery, space, and capital as well as other qualitative influences, the difference was between privatistic and communal traditions that were deeply rooted in these two local cultures. Virginia, from its inception, was characterized by acquisitiveness and a concern for the freedom of the individual as Edmund Morgan recently has shown so well, while the early settlement of Massachusetts tended to elevate the good of the community over the individual. These traditions were undergoing important changes, particularly in the Massachusetts towns and above all in Salem, where the impact of modernization was keenly felt. But in some respects the changes accentuated older traditions. In Virginia, the separation of church and state further liberated the individual from restraints both upon his conscience and his pocketbook. That this did not occur in Massachusetts, and that Article III of the Massachusetts Constitution which preserved tax support for religion was strenuously urged by Samuel Adams, the arch-radical of the resistance in Massachusetts, demonstrated both the force of tradition and the susceptibility of republican ideology to sharply different interpretations. Ironically, the process of modernization itself was not entirely incompatible with the older emphasis upon community—for government promotion, if not of religion, then of education, streets, and even welfare, was desirable for the improvement of the environment in which modernized individuals could realize themselves.

IV

Assuming as I have that these different local political cultures affected, if they did not entirely dominate, the deliberations of the Continental Congress, what were their implications for the nationalization of American politics? How might these libertarian, but static, and communal, but modernizing, polities converge in the first national legislature?

It is not very difficult to see the posture of the New England delegations in the Continental Congress during the early phases of the war as corporate, republican town politics writ large. The aggressive stance of New Englanders such as Samuel Adams who complained from Philadelphia in 1777 about the "lethargy" of the Pennsylvanians, and who was ready to "give up this City and State for lost until recovered by other Americans," was symbolic of that ideology of regenerative republicanism that seemed to make some sense in the aroused localities of Massachusetts, but which was less applicable to the pluralistic culture of the middle states or, as events were to demonstrate, to the diffuse communities of Virginia. Military exertion, according the the faintly reactionary-rural republican world view of the New Englanders, should emanate from the community rather than from the desire for prominence or profit. Thus bounties raised by the town for enlistment of common soldiers were commendable, but pensions for officers were "debasing." Accordingly, New Englanders in the Congress almost uniformly opposed half pay for officers for life while most Southerners and middle states delegates supported pensions. As Thomas Burke, delegate from North Carolina put it, "The arguments drawn from Patriotism and public spirit may be fine . . ., but I choose to trust to some principle of more certain, lasting and powerful influence. . . ."

The pronounced opposition of the New Englanders to French influence in Congressional politics may have derived partly from republican purism associated with the idealized homogeneous community. Of course the fact that the French ministers Gérard and Luzerne opposed American claims to the fisheries gave the New Englanders ample cause for their anti-Gallicanism, but New England criticism of Gérard and Jay, his candidate for minister to negotiate the peace—a "Lickspittle" and a "Perfidious Jesuit"—was an elaborate orchestration of the perils of contaminating the republican experiment with outside, foreign support.

For most Southerners in the Continental Congress, the Lees being a decided exception, French influence was welcome. Meriwether Smith of Essex County, Virginia, went so far as to join Gouverneur Morris of New York in presenting a resolution actually drawn up by Gérard. The pro-French stand of the Southern delegations is reasonably understandable in terms of their local political cultures. The diffuseness of Southern societies which made them particularly vulnerable to British military pressure did, in fact, render Southern government almost "imbecilic" as Jefferson protested it was not, or should not be. It was natural for Southerners in Congress to turn to the French for assistance, just as it was natural for them to advocate discrimination against British shipping in both the Continental and Federal Congresses.

Excepting the Lees, the Virginians followed a policy toward Robert Morris and his program that was perfectly intelligible in terms of their local circumstances. During the days of peril in 1781 they were active supporters of the move to give Morris almost anything he demanded as conditions for accepting the newly created Superintendency of Finance. The situation was altered, however, when in 1783 Morris recommended and James Wilson proposed a general fund under Congressional administration. What Morris and middle states delegates were offering was a system that would achieve nationalization of American politics, not through regeneration, but through interest— specifically, the interest of investors in the national debt.

This starkly different kind of appeal worried New Englanders who viewed it as a conspiracy against republican institutions rather than as a pragmatic way to strengthen the union and benefit security-holders. Actually, some New Englanders were sympathetic with a general fund, but they objected to the men and the influences, including the military, that had combined to press the program upon Congress. For different reasons, the Virginian delegates opposed Morris's program. They were particularly concerned about taxes on land and slaves in Morris's original report. Even the proposal for a 5 percent impost, endorsed by Southerners during the war crisis, became suspect in peace, and the Virginia assembly rescinded its previous acceptance of the duty. The opposition in Congress and in the states from both New England and the South was too much for the pragmatic middle states nationalists who left Congress, not to return to national politics until it was time for a new government.

But neither the Easterners nor the Virginians had given up on the Confederation. There were other ways to meld the union. The West still existed as a powerful lure to land-hungry Americans. Indeed, its availability was virtually indispensable for Virginians if they were to continue to live as they had in the past. The Virginia delegates during the middle eighties followed two new avenues to a nationalization of American politics that, although they were not entirely compatible, were expressive of Virginia's local values. One was the cession of Virginia's vast claims north of the Ohio, and the subsequent organization of the Western territory in a way that would be attractive to prospective settlers. The other was to simultaneously draw a revenue from imports and strike at the ancient oppressor, England, by granting Congress much more ample powers over external commerce. The western policy was famously successful. The land ordinances strengthened the union and at the same time embodied encouraging compromises between the New England corporate way and the more individualistic Southern technique of occupying the land. The other project of regulating commerce was proposed by James Monroe as an amendment to Article 9 of the Confederation and was designed to regulate foreign and coastal trade and levy discriminatory import duties. This was totally unsuccessful, for it never left Congress. It was shortly overshadowed by the bitterly divisive Jay-Gardoqui negotiations that pitted Northern commercial and Southern expansive interests against each other in a manner that threatened to break the union. The management of trade proved to be something Congress was unable to handle effectively. This demonstrated the incapacity of Congress, for it would be a conference on trade outside Congress that brought forth the Constitutional Convention.

The nationalization of American politics was a necessary process in the aftermath of a colonial revolution. It was not completed by the Continental Congress which sometimes deflected, sometimes subsumed, but sometimes aggravated the strains that accompany the integration of disparate colonial polities. During the Federal decade sharp struggles continued over the location of the national capital, a national system of finance, trade policies toward England and France, and other matters that seemed to echo the partisan politics of the Continental Congress. But in the process the strains tended to abate as sectional politics were broken down in a legislature that was more sensitive to the varied concerns of an increasingly diversified nation.

Paradoxically, it was the Virginians who best articulated the libertarian ideology that would draw adherents from all reas of the nation, at the same time that it was the South that most retained its colonial character. Ironically, one of the areas that best reflected the acquisitive individualism associated with modernizing America was the third middle district of Massachusetts which tended still to cling to its older rural-republican world view. The complexity of the process, marked by divergence not only between the colonial parts of the new nation but also the perceptions of what those parts were, reminds us of how successful, in the end, the republican experiment was.